INTRODUCTION

A view of the city and, below, the Castle.

"The Magical City", "The Golden City", "The City of a Hundred Towers", the "Paris of the East"; these are just some of the most common definitions adopted by popular tourist publications when describing Prague, a city of around 1,200,000 inhabitants and, since 1st January 1993, capital of the Czech Republic, as well as capital of central Bohemia. The city offers a wealth of architectural, artistic and cultural treasures, and possesses an individual charm: buildings everywhere are of pleasing architectural form and proportional harmony, with close attention to ornamental detail. It lies proudly along the banks of the River Vltava (also know as the Moldau), amid the gentle surroundings of the hills which characterise this part of Bohemia.

Prague has been a melting-pot of ethnic groups since ancient times, existing by combining Czech elements with Jewish and German ones, and allowing the development of religious movements, trade and commerce, and industry, thanks to its favourable geographic position on the communication routes between Central and Eastern Europe, and between the North and South of the

vast German and Slavonic area. A jealous keeper of its mysteries, the city is reluctant to reveal itself to the curiosity of those wanting to unearth the secrets of the alchemists of the past. The birthplace or one time residence of many famous people, such as the astronomers Tycho Brahe and Johannes Kepler, the Dientzenhofers, Albert Einstein, Wolfgang Amadeus Mozart, Antonín Dvořák, Bedřich Smetana, Jaroslav Hašek, Franz Kafka, Charles IV, Jan Hus, St John Nepomuk, and many other illustrious figures, the city bears witness to cultures and civilisations from all over the world.

Over the centuries Prague has survived wars and disasters, but its charm has remained unchanged. The artistic and cultural treasures of Prague are unchanged and intact while its beautiful monuments are rich in history.

It is fascinating to walk from the Castle buildings to Charles Bridge or from Malá Strana to the Jewish district, wandering along romantic little streets steeped in a magical atmosphere, passing from the Middle Ages to late Baroque times and returning to the present with the most up-to-date services and activities.

Staré Město
Old Town

CHARLES STREET
Karlova ulice

This is a very old street that was on the route of the coronation processions and it still has an unmistakable charm. It is flanked by several beautiful Gothic and Renaissance buildings many of which have been converted into hotels, restaurants and shops where visitors are enraptured by the picturesque atmosphere. The elegant architecture and original decorations are a magnificent backdrop for a delightful walk to discover yet another enchanting corner of Prague.

CLAM-GALLAS PALACE
Clam-Gallasův palác

In the southern part of *Mariánské náměstí* stands Clam-Gallas Palace, a splendid example of Baroque art, designed by the Viennese J. B. Fischer von Erlach.
The building now houses the **Prague city archives**. M. Braun and C. Carlone were among those who contributed to the decoration of the palace with sculptures and paintings.
Note the 19th century *Vtlava Fountain* by V. Prachner, situated close to the wall of the courtyard.

Some of the decorations that adorn this very picturesque street.
Left, the original decoration on the House "at the Golden Tiger".

The Clam-Gallas Palace: a detail of the "Giants" on either side of the portal.

The typical shops along Karlova ulice are housed in elegant buildings.

THE GOLDEN BOOK
PRAGUE

BONECHI

Distributed by:

NEPALA, spol. s r.o. Horňátecká 1772/19, 182 00 Praha 8, Česká republika
Tel.:+420 284 686 704 - Fax: +420 284 686 606
Mobil: +420 775 368 449 - +420 602 368 449
E-mail: nepala@bonechi.cz - Internet: www.bonechi.cz

Concept and project: Casa Editrice Bonechi
Editorial management: Monica Bonechi
Graphic concept: Monica Bonechi
Graphic design and cover: Manuela Ranfagni
Editing: Federica Balloni
Texts: Giuliano Valdes *with* Federica Balloni *and* Patrizia Fabbri.
Text on pages 94-95: Maria Novella Batini
Drawing pages 24-25: Sauro Giampaia

© Copyright 2009
by Casa Editrice Bonechi, Via Cairoli 18/b, Florence - Italy
E-mail: bonechi@bonechi.it

Printed in Italy by Centro Stampa Editoriale Bonechi - *Sesto Fiorentino.*

The photographs in this book are the property of the Casa Editrice Bonechi Archives
and were taken by Marco Bonechi *and* Andrea Pistolesi.

Other sources:
© Picture Library of Prague Castle: *pages 67 top (left and right).*
© Jewish Museum in Prague: *pages 29, 30, 31, 33.*

The photographs on pages 3, 16-17, 19 top and right, 27 top left, 28 bottom, 35 centre, 36-37, 44-46, 48, 59 bottom right, 61 bottom, 68 bottom, 80 bottom, courtesy of Anatol Nepala.

The publisher apologizes for any errors or omissions of attribution and is ready to compensate parties holding rights to the photographs.

ISBN 978-88-476-2405-4
www.bonechi.com

Some of the buildings in this district.
Top right, one of the many beautiful stores
along Karlova ulice, one of the city's main
shopping streets.

The façade of Rott House and a glimpse
of Seminářská Street.

OLD TOWN SQUARE
Staroměstské náměstí

This huge square is the thriving heart of old Prague. Its historical importance, on the right bank of the Vtlava, can be compared to that of the Castle on the opposite side of the river. *Staroměstské náměstí* is not merely an impressive blend of architectural styles and monuments; it represents the very essence of the city itself. It has been the setting for the many events, both happy and tragic, which have marked Prague's long history: in 1422 the preacher J. Želivský was executed here (a plaque commemorates the event); in 1621 the leaders of the Protestant revolt were executed (see commemorative plaque); in 1915 the bronze *Jan Hus Monument* was inaugurated, on the occasion of the 5th centenary of his death (the work is by L. Šaloun, and an epigraph reads *Love and be truthful to each other*); in 1945 the people of Prague joyfully welcomed the Soviet army at the end of the Second World War; in 1968 the crowd bombarded Soviet tanks with Molotov cocktails for shattering the dream of the "Prague Spring", and the Hus Monument was veiled as a sign of mourning. The square at night, with its carefully studied illumination, is especially charming: the lights create surreal, fantastic, almost fairy-tale dimensions on the façades of the noble buildings and up towards the incredible spires of the **Church of Our Lady of Týn**. All around, in the square and along *Karlova*, jugglers and musicians brighten the city's evenings, again offering a typically "Parisian" image.

A magnificent view from the tower of the Staré Město town hall towards Staroměstské náměstí and the city that seems dominated by the spires of the bell towers of the Church of Our Lady of Týn.

OLD TOWN HALL
Staroměstská radnice

The history of this building begins in the 12th century and continues uninterrupted, through various periods of extension, damage, destruction and reconstruction, right up until the last restoration work carried out between 1978 and 1981. The original central part of the building was constructed in 1338; a tower was then added in 1364. **Kříž House** was built before this, in 1360, and is particulary notable for its lively paintwork and the epigraph *Praga caput regni*. Serious damage was inflicted on the complex at the end of the Second World War. The **Council Chamber** has maintained its Gothic

Staré Město Town Hall and its tower seem from the old city square, and a detail of the building.

character which originates from the second half of the 15th century. The huge **Meeting Hall** contains paintings by V. Brožík (*Jiří z Poděbrad elected King of Bohemia, J. Hus before the Council of Constance*). There is a charming view from the top of the 69m high **Old Town Hall Tower**, which can be reached by lift.

ASTRONOMICAL CLOCK
Orloj

The clock was built by Master Mikuláš of Kadaň and was mounted in the lower part of the Old Town Hall Tower at the beginning of the 15th century. At the end of the century Master Hanuš of Růže was responsible for its rebuilding, and in the second half of the 16th century it was perfected and enlarged by J. Táborský. Every hour the charming *Procession of Apostles* appears with its eloquent allegories, attracting the surprised attention of tourists and visitors who crowd round in the attractive little square below.

The upper face of the Astronomical Clock showing old Bohemian Time, real time, the visible portion of the sky divided into twelve parts and the paths of the sun and moon through the twelve signs of the zodiac.

A view of the Astronomical Clock in its entirety.

The figures on the sides of the lower face of the Astronomical Clock portray four virtues.

The figures on the sides of the upper face represent vanity, greed, death and lust (bottom).

CHURCH OF OUR LADY OF TÝN

Kostel Panny Marie před Týnem

This mighty construction, one of the capital's most famous symbols, rises high above the rooftops of old Prague. The present day building was erected on the site of an earlier Romanesque church in the second half of the 14th century, and the choir was completed towards the end of that century. The **façade,** in all its austere, Gothic magnificence, was completed in the second half of the 15th century at the request of Jiří of Poděbrady.

The tympanum contains a *Statue of the Madonna*, and the façade is dominated by twin *bell towers*, although these were built at different times (the northern one in the 15th century and the southern one in the 16th century). They are both 80m high and crowned with soaring pinnacles and angular turrets which contribute to the fairy-tale setting. The high, majestic **interior** is distinguished by the mighty pillars which separate the three naves and support the imposing ogival arches. The ceiling above the naves is formed of cross-vaults. Fine wooden *altars* with gold-leaf work stand against the pillars. The Church also contains the *Tomb of Tycho Brahe*, Court Astronomer to Rudolph II; a Gothic *Madonna and Child* (15th century); and the late-Gothic canopy by M. Rejsek (late 15th century). The paintings on the high altar (*Holy Trinity and Assumption of the Virgin*) are by Karel Škréta (17th century).

The majestic Church of Our Lady of Týn, with its pointed bell towers dominates the historic centre and spectacular square of Staré Město. A detail of the church façade showing the tympanum and statue of the Virgin Mary.

A breathtaking view of the rooftops of Staré Město from the Town Hall tower.

The Storch House is richly decorated with sgraffito work; a painting of St. Wenceslas on horseback by Mikoláš Aleš adorns the façade.

HOUSE 'AT THE GOLDEN UNICORN'
U Zlatého jednorožce

This building, at n° 20, was extended as early as the 14th century, and towards the end of the following century it was rebuilt in late-Gothic style. The **façade** bears the hallmark of the late Baroque period and dates from the 18th century. A plaque here commemorates the famous composer, B. Smetana, who opened his first music school in this house.

STORCH HOUSE
Štorchův dům

This lovely building, situated at the southern side of the square at n° 16, close to *Celetná ulice*, is distinguished by its beautiful decorations and the architectural details which ennoble the fine **façade**. The painting which adorns the façade, and which recalls the type of fresco-decorated houses common among the aristocratic residences of central Europe, depicts *St Wenceslas on horseback*. Originally a 14th-15th century Gothic residence, Storch House was restored in Neo-Renaissance style towards the end of the 19th century and remains as such today. The building next door, known as the **House 'at the Stone Ram'** (n° 17), is also called *At the Unicorn* after the subject of the bas-relief which decorates the façade.

Top right, a detail of the Kříž House showing the inscription 'Praga caput regni' above an elegant window. Below, some of the historical buildings around the Staré Město square, including the "House of the Minute" that is richly decorated with sgraffito work.

Left, other fine buildings facing onto the Staré Město square: the House at the Golden Unicorn, the House at the Stone Ram and Storch House, the first, fourth and fifth on the right, respectively.

GOLTZ-KINSKÝ PALACE
Palác Goltz-Kinských

This impressive late Baroque palace, which enlivens the eastern side of the square with its Rococo and neo-classical designs, was created when a Romanesque building and an early Gothic house were joined together. Count J. E. Goltz entrusted the project to K. I. Dientzenhofer, while the actual building work was carried out by A. Lurago in the latter half of the 18th century. It was subsequently acquired by Prince R. Kinský. Note the **façade** and its interesting features: the pilasters, the triangular tympanums, the long balcony resting on the columns situated on either side of the portals, the windows decorated with stuccowork and Rococo patterns, and the statues situated on the attic. The palace houses the **Permanent Exhibition of Bohemian Landscape Painting of the National Gallery in Prague**.

HOUSE 'AT THE STONE BELL'
Dům 'U kamenného zvonu'

The building's elegant Gothic **façade** was only rediscovered in the 1960s when some reconstruction work brought it to light underneath a dubious late 19th-century addition. The origins of the house date back to the 13th century, and its name is already mentioned in 15th century records. Its appearance was then gradually altered until no trace remained of the beautiful building which, however, visitors can now appreciate once more.

Above, a view of the square with the facades of Goltz-Kinský palace and the House "at the Stone Bell".

Left, the tympanum of the Goltz-Kinský palace with the bell towers of the Church of Our Lady of Týn in the background.

Below, from the left, a detail of the beautiful Art Nouveau building, headquarters of the offices for local development, the House "at the Stone Bell," and the Gothic portal of the former School of Týn, that leads into the church of the same name.

Church of St Nicholas in Staré Město
Kostel svatého Mikuláše

This masterpiece of Baroque architecture was built in the first half of the 18th century by K. I. Dientzenhofer. The monumental south-facing **façade** is a triumph of exquisite Baroque architectural and ornamental patterns. The twin bell towers, the dome and the central part of the façade are of singular elegance. The **interior** consists of a central nave with side **chapels**. The ceiling is decorated with scenes from the *Lives of St Nicholas and St Benedict,* and the frescoes in the side chapels and presbytery are the work of P. Asam the Elder. The *Statue of St Nicholas* on the side façade was added at the beginning of the 20th century and is by B. Šimonovský.

The Church of Saint Nicholas at Staré Město, a masterpiece of Baroque architecture. Above, the elegant dome and a night time view.

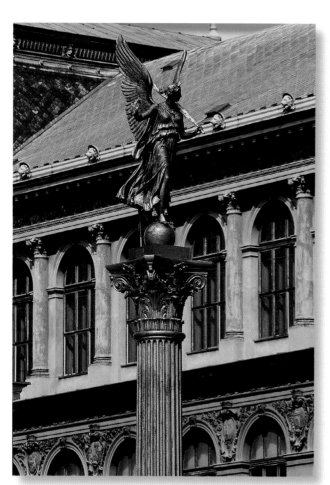

RUDOLFINUM - HOUSE OF ARTISTS
Dům umělců

This grandiose construction, with its elegant architectural forms, stands majestically on the banks of the Vltava and overlooks the square named after *Jan Palach*, the martyr of the 'Prague Spring'. It is also known as the *Rudolfinum*, as it was named in honour of Rudolph of Habsburg. It was built in the second half of the 19th century by J. Zítek and J. Schulz. Once the seat of the Czechoslovak Parliament (1919-1939), it is considered to be one of the most outstanding examples of neo-Renaissance architecture in Prague and hosts the annual opening of the Festival of classical music, the *Prague Spring*. An allegory dedicated to Wagner adorns the main entrance, while the balustrade is decorated with statues of illustrious artists and musicians. The **Dvořák Room** is particularly interesting with its fine decorations, dedicated to this famous composer as is the statue in front of the building. Close to the river is the *Statue of Josef Mánes*, by B. Kafka (1951). The nearby *Mánesův most* is also named after this Czech artist.

This graceful winged figure rises on the Náměstí Jana Palacha and is an elegant ornament of the Rudolfinum.

The beautiful Rudolfinum overlooks the vast Náměstí Jana Palacha.

A view of the Křižovnické náměstí and the statue of Charles IV (1848). Right, a detail.

KNIGHT OF THE CROSS SQUARE
Křižovnické náměstí

This square opens out from the eastern end of Charles Bridge. It was created in the 16th century and was part of the route followed by the coronation processions of the Bohemian sovereigns.

It is distinguished by the *Statue of Charles IV*, cast in iron in the first half of the 19th century.

CHARLES IV

Emperor of the Holy Roman Empire, but also king of the Romans, king of Bohemia, count of Luxembourg and margrave of Brandenburg, this son of John of Luxembourg and Elisabeth of Bohemia was christened Wenceslas on his birth on 14 May 1316 and only took the name Charles at the time of his coronation. The first wife of Charles IV, rigorously of royal blood, was Blanche of Valois, a half sister of Philippe IV of France, who gave him two daughters – Margaret and Catherine. The second was Anne, daughter of Rudolph II of the Palatinate; the third, Anne of Schweidnitz, was the mother of Wenceslas. The fourth was Elizabeth of Pomerania whom he married in 1363 and who was mother to Anne, Sigmund – the future German emperor, king of Bohemia and Hungary, and margrave of Brandenburg – John and Margaret. Certainly a numerous and complicated family, but one that not only supported him when emperor but still accompany him in his eternal and monumental resting place.

The exterior of the baroque Church of Saint Francis Seraphicus at the Knights of the Cross and a detail of the lavishly decorated interior.

From *Křižovnické náměstí*, on one side of the church some steps lead down to the level of the river where the arch of the old Judith Bridge (*Juditin Most*) can still be seen. An attractive little spot for tourists offers boat trips.

CHURCH OF ST FRANCIS SERAPHICUS AT THE KNIGHTS OF THE CROSS
Kostel sv. Františka Serafinského

The plans for this Baroque church were drawn up by J. B. Mathey, and building was completed in the second half of the 17th century. The temple, which was built on the site of an earlier Gothic church, is distinguished by its elegant dome and its **façade**, inspired by French Pre-Classicism. The statues near the entrance (*Madonna* and *St John Nepomuk*) are by M. W. Jäckel. Other sculptures on the façade represent *Angels* and *Patron Saints of Bohemia*. The **interior** is richly decorated, and the dome bears a fresco of the *Last Judgement* by V. V. Reiner (18th century). The nearby *Vintners' Column* bears a *Statue of St Wenceslas* (17th century).

Church of the Holy Saviour
Kostel sv. Salvátora

This church, once part of the *Clementinum* (situated next to the church), is a Jesuit temple, built between the 16th and 17th centuries in Renaissance style. The porch in front of the main portal was added in the 17th century by C. Lurago and F. Caratti; the sculptures and vases which decorate it are the work of J. J. Bendl. The addition of the towers in the 18th century marked the completion of the church's construction. The **interior** boasts a 17th century ceiling fresco (*The Four Quarters of the World*, by K. Kovář).

Clementinum
Klementinum

Formerly the Jesuit College, this building is considered to be the most impressive architectural complex in the capital, after the Castle. An entire district, including elegant homes, churches and gardens, was demolished in the second half of the 16th century in order to make way for the complex. The reason for this was to support the Jesuit apostolate in their efforts to expand and consolidate Catholicism in Prague. This grandiose scheme of urban reconstruction was planned by F. Caratti and F. M. Kaňka. The 17th century main **façade** is decorated with stucco ornaments and busts of *Roman Emperors*. The **interior** houses the **National Library** (numbering more than six million volumes, 6000 manuscripts, including the valuable *Vyšehrad Codex*, and 4000 incunabula). The *Hall of the Jesuit Library* is decorated with

A detail of the Baroque façade of the Church of the Holy Saviour, decorated with thirteen statues and five vases.

ceiling frescoes (*Biblical themes, Muses*); *the Mozart Hall* and the former *Chapel of Mirrors* are noted for their pictorial decoration; the *Hall of Mathematics* contains a collection of globes and antique table clocks. Also of interest, in the south-western courtyard (not always open), is the *Statue of the Prague Student*, in memory of those who defended the Charles Bridge at the end of the Thirty Years' War.

The Clementinum from the Astronomical Tower.

The interior of the Chapel of Mirrors, completed by F. M. Kaňka in 1724. The walls are decorated with fine stuccowork, elegant mirrors and four figures of saints by V. V. Reiner. The ceiling paintings, probably by Jan Hiebl, depict scenes from the life of the Virgin Mary. The chapel was deconsecrated in 1784, it was rededicated and used for worship for a short time around 1816 and is now an exhibition and concert hall.

Left, a section of one of the rooms in the National Library; the ceiling was splendidly frescoed by Jan Hiebl in 1727.

Some details of the interior of the Astronomical Tower, which, in the past served as the seat of the Astronomical Observatory of the Clementinium. The telescopes were positioned at the corner apertures and stood on steel supports. Today, the top of the tower can be reached via an old wooden staircase. Along the climb there are display cabinets containing interesting antique astronomical instruments. The climb is rewarded by a beautiful view of the entire city.

Josefov
Jewish Quarter

Prague's old Jewish Ghetto (*Židovské ghetto*) occupies part of the Staré Město quarter and is important both in terms of its size, and the cultural and tourist interest it provides. The *Josefov* quarter takes its name from the Emperor Joseph II. The first Jewish settlements in Prague appeared around the 10th century, and by the 17th century more than 7000 Jews had made the city their home. Persecutions, fires and plundering were regular occurrences

Klaus Synagogue
page 27

Ceremonial Hall

Břehová

17. listopadu

Břehová

U starého hřbitova

U staré

Old Jewish Cemetery
page 27

Valentinská

Široká

Široká

Žatecká

Pinkas Synagogue
page 31

Kaprova

throughout the centuries, making life difficult for the Jewish community. Towards the middle of the 18th century Maria Theresa of Habsburg decreed that the Jews should be driven out. Later that century, however, the Emperor Joseph II had the walls of the Ghetto demolished, restoring both the Jewish quarter itself, and its administrative status. The area was named Josefov in his honour. Jews were not granted civil rights until 1848. The period of Nazi occupation in Prague (1939-1945) was the darkest time for the Jewish community whose members became the object of persecution and deportation. It is estimated that 90 per cent of Bohemian and Moravian Jews were killed during the Second World War. Used for religious and non-religious purposes, the group of buildings which make up the Ghetto together with the **cemetery**, has now been transformed into a kind of large open-air museum. One of the most beautiful architectural features of the Ghetto is the **Jewish Town Hall** (*Židovská radnice*),

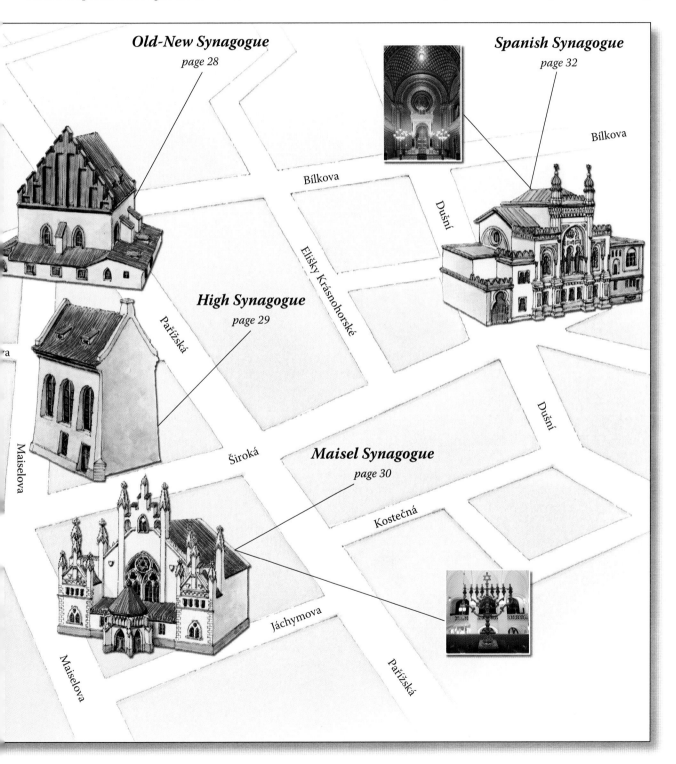

Old-New Synagogue

page 28

Spanish Synagogue

page 32

Bílkova

Bílkova

Dušní

High Synagogue

page 29

Pařížská

Eliśky Krásnohorské

Dušní

Maiselova

Široká

Maisel Synagogue

page 30

Kostečná

Maiselova

Jáchymova

Pařížská

A detail of the Ceremonial Hall, a new-Romanesque building designed by the architect J. Gerstl (1906-1908) for holding funeral services. Today it houses the Jewish Museum.

A detail of the Jewish Town Hall, with its two clocks, one on the tower and one on the tympanum with Hebrew numbers and hands that move counter-clockwise.

a Renaissance building which dates from the second half of the 16th century. It was remodelled in Baroque style in the latter half of the 18th century, and extended at the beginning of the 20th century. Note the unusual clock situated in the tympanum, under the small clock tower: it has Hebrew figures and the hands move counter-clockwise.

JEWISH MUSEUM
Židovské muzeum v Praze

The collections which make up the framework of the museum, and which allow us to understand the development of the city's Jewish community and its culture, originate from various synagogues in Bohemia, Moravia, and Europe in general. Despite the fact that the Nazis wanted to make it into the 'Exotic museum of an extinct race', the number of exhibits increased considerably precisely during the period of the occupation of Prague.

Franz Kafka

Franz Kafka was born in Prague in 1883, son of a middle-class Jewish family. After he earned his law degree he worked for an insurance company and only cultivated his passion for writing during his free time. Although a Czech, his novels and stories were written in German and are among the most outstanding works of 20th century literature (such as *The Trial, The Castle* and *The Metamorphosis*). During his lifetime he only published a few stories, the majority of his works were published posthumously. Kafka died in Vienna in 1924 and was buried in the New Jewish Cemetery at Strašnice in Prague.

The bronze statue of Frank Kafka, by Jaroslav Róna.

The bronze plaque in memory of the great writer, outside the house where he was born, at the corner of Maiselova street and Frank Kafka Square.

Old Jewish Cemetery
Starý židovský hřbitov

The feature which makes this site so interesting, and one of the places most visited by tourists, is the incredible number of gravestones it holds (12,000 tombstones, for more than 100,000 people buried here). Because of the lack of available space, they are all packed tightly together, stone upon stone in a picturesque fashion, giving the place a fascinating atmosphere. It is said that in some parts of the cemetery there are at least nine layers of burials. The Hebrew epigraphs and the relief sculpting which decorates the tombstones give an interesting insight into the Jewish community of the time, since, apart from the sex and marital status of the deceased, they also record connections with a particular art, trade or social class of any importance, such as that of a rabbi. The cemetery, which was founded in the first half of the 15th century, continued to be used as such at least until the second half of the 18th century.

Klaus Synagogue
Klausova synagoga

The name of this synagogue derives from the term *klausen*, which refers to Jewish prayer houses. In fact the 17th century Klaus Synagogue is built on the site once occupied by the Jewish School of Löw ben Bezalel, a 16th century Rabbi and philosopher. The Baroque building houses a collection of prints and manuscripts.

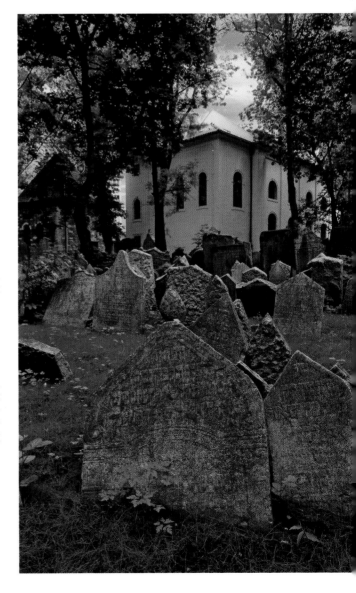

The Klaus Synagogue seen from the Old Jewish Cemetery with its amazing overlapping tombstones.

Left, the statue of Moses by F. Bílek (1905) stands in the garden of the Old-New Synagogue.

OLD-NEW SYNAGOGUE
Staronová synagoga

This synagogue, originally Gothic in design, was extended in Cistercian Gothic style in the 13th century. Further modifications and additions were completed between the 15th and 18th centuries. Renovation and restoration work was also carried out in the 19th-20th centuries. Considered the oldest in Europe, the synagogue is still used for religious services. A *Statue of Moses* by F. Bílek can be seen in the adjoining **park**.

The outside of the High Synagogue, at the top we can see one of the clocks on the Jewish Town Hall.

The subdued interior of the High Synagogue with the bimah in the centre. Today the synagogue is also used by the Jewish Community of Prague for other activities.

An interesting view of the Old-New Synagogue, the oldest synagogue in Europe.

HIGH SYNAGOGUE
Vysoká synagoga

The High Synagogue was built in the second half of the 16th century, to a design by P. Roder. In the 19th century restoration was carried out to separate it from the **Town Hall**. The central, square hall, originally Renaissance in style, was transformed in the 17th-19th centuries and remodelled in neo-Renaissance style. Note the magnificent stellar vaulting. The rooms of the synagogue are used for exhibitions by the **Jewish Museum** (they contain vestments, manuscripts and precious ornaments). The High Synagogue is closed to the public. Tourists can visit only the ground floor of the building.

MAISEL SYNAGOGUE
Maiselova synagoga

The synagogue takes its name from the mayor of the Jewish quarter at the time of Rudolph II, Mordechai Maisel, for whom it was originally created as a private chapel. It was built in Renaissance style at the end of the 16th century, and reconstructed in Baroque style about a century later, after a fire. The building as it appears today was restored in neo-Gothic style between the 19th and 20th centuries. The synagogue now houses an exhibition on the *History of the Jews in Bohemia and Moravia from the 10th to 18th centuries*, from the **Jewish Museum**.

A plaque commemorating Mordechai Maisel, the founder, inside the synagogue.

An interesting view of the Maisel Synagogue from the gallery. In the foreground, a fine gilded nine-arm candelabrum.

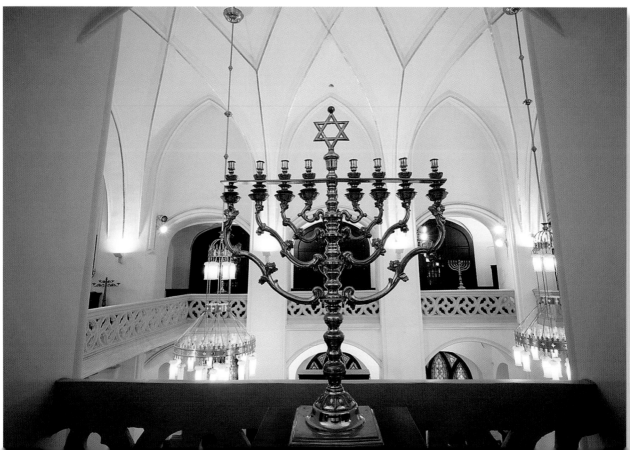

PINKAS SYNAGOGUE
Pinkasova synagoga

The earliest religious building on the site of today's Pinkas Synagogue, probably a ritual bath (*mikva*), is said to date from the 11th-12th centuries. In the first half of the 16th century a late-Gothic synagogue was constructed in the building which had been the home of Rabbi Pinkas (for whom it is named). This was rebuilt and enlarged in the first half of the 17th century, in late Renaissance style. In the 1950s the synagogue became the seat of the *Memorial of the 77, 297,* a monument erected in memory of the victims of the Holocaust.

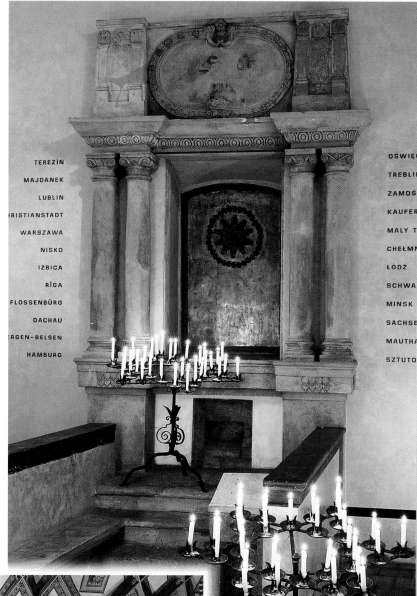

TEREZÍN
MAJDANEK
LUBLIN
RISTIANSTADT
WARSZAWA
NISKO
IZBICA
RĪGA
FLOSSENBÜRG
DACHAU
ERGEN-BELSEN
HAMBURG

OŚWIĘ
TREBLI
ZAMOŚ
KAUFER
MALY T
CHEŁMN
ŁÓDŹ
SCHWA
MINSK
SACHSE
MAUTHA
SZTUTO

A detail of the ceiling in the Pinkas Synagogue with its late-Gothic arches. The grate of the bimah repeats the Star of David motif with the hat in the middle (symbol of the Jewish Community of Prague).

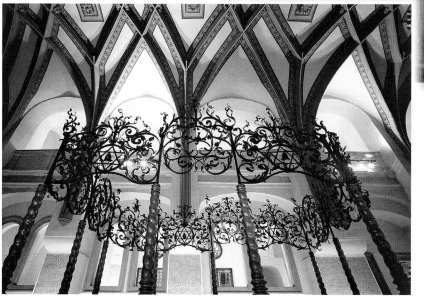

The early Baroque style Aron Hakodesh in the Pinkas Synagogue. On either side are inscriptions with the names of the concentration and extermination camps to which most of the Czech Jews were deported.

The western façade of the Spanish Synagogue with its rich Moorish decorations.

The interior of the Spanish Synagogue that is richly decorated with materials and patterns that recalls the Alhambra in Granada.

SPANISH SYNAGOGUE
Španělská synagoga

The building which today houses the Spanish Synagogue bears some striking Moorish features, added in the second half of the 19th century.

The temple interior is strongly reminiscent of the Alhambra in Granada. The synagogue owes its name to a community of Iberian Jews who came to Prague to escape persecution.

Occupying the site of the **Old School**, the oldest synagogue in the city (12th century), it has been destroyed by fire and rebuilt several times.

Nové Město
New Town

NA PŘÍKOPĚ STREET
Na Příkopě

Situated at the heart of the *Golden Cross*, this street is Prague's lively commercial centre, full of shops, banks, restaurants and office blocks. Its Czech name means 'on the ditch' (in fact, *Na Příkopě* lies along the path of a moat which divided *Staré Město* - the 'Old Town' - from *Nové Město* - the 'New Town'); in the past, before it was filled in, all manner of rubbish was thrown in here and it was therefore actually a ditch filled with sewage. At n° 4 is the 19th century building which houses **Dům elegance**, the oldest department store in the Capital (*Koruna*). At n° 10 is the **Sylva-Taroucca Palace**, a splendid example of Bohemian Baroque architecture. Also worthy of note are the **Casa Slava**, originally Baroque in design (17th-18th centuries) and renovated in neo-Classical style at the end of the 19th century (now a modern shopping centre), and the **State Bank Building** at n° 24, erected in the late 1930s. Previously on this site stood some famous hotels where illustrious figures of the 19th century used to stay.

WENCESLAS SQUARE
Václavské náměstí

The impressive *Wenceslas Square* is situated in the heart of the city. Its dimensions (750 x 60m) make it look more like a Parisian *Boulevard* than a square. It is a lively conglomeration of well-known hotels (like the 'Evropa' at n° 25, a treasure of Art Nouveau architecture), restaurants and cafés, galleries, shops, cinemas and clubs, which together with *Na Příkopě, Na Můstku* and *28.října* forms the group of main thoroughfares known as the *Golden Cross*. This is the commercial heart of the Czech metropolis, redeveloped in the 1980s to include wide green spaces, following the building of the underground system. In the square, opposite the **National Museum of Prague**, stands the *St Wenceslas Monument*, the work of J. V. Myslbek (1912-1913). The patron saint of Bohemia is represented on horseback, surrounded by the statues of *St Ludmila, St Procopius, St Adalbert* and *St Agnes of Prague*. The square was originally founded as a horse market by Charles IV, at the same time as Nové Město; it

Saint Wenceslas Square facing the National Museum of Prague.

was given its present name towards the middle of the 19th century. Wenceslas Square also represents the moral and historical conscience of the newly-formed Czech Republic. In the early months of 1969 it was the scene of dramatic events following the military occupation by troops of the Warsaw Pact (August 1968). On 16th January the Philosophy student Jan Palach burnt himself to death at the foot of the St Wenceslas Monument, and a few weeks later the student Jan Zajíc committed suicide in the same square. Nineteen years later, on 28 October 1988, the Communist police forcefully dispersed a demonstration commemorating the proclamation of the First Republic. Again in 1989 there were further incidents of brutality against demonstrators commemorating the sacrifice of Palach. These events led inevitably to the 'Velvet Revolution' which, within a few months, restored the dignity of a free country to Czechoslovakia.

CHURCH OF OUR LADY
OF THE SNOWS
Kostel Panny Marie Sněžné

This church was built under the patronage of Charles IV, who in 1347 wanted it to be the place of his coronation. Once completed the ambitious projects was to have been even more magnificent than the Cathedral of St Vitus. The 30m high choir had been completed by the end of the century. The magnificent Gothic portal on the north side is decorated with an abundance of statues of saints. With the coming of the 15th century the church began its gradual decline; the ceiling collapsed during the first half of the 17th and was replaced with another in Renaissance style. This church was also the meeting place of the Hussite movement. One of the outstanding features **inside** the church is the 17th century Baroque high altar, the largest altar of its kind in Prague's churches.

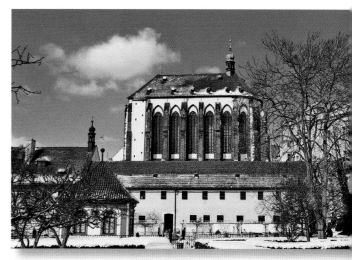

JINDŘIŠSKÁ TOWER
Jindřišská věž

This tower dates from the late Gothic period (1472-1476), after the fire of 1745 it was rebuilt in the Baroque style and then was remodelled, again in Gothic style. The *clock* dates from 1577. The Jindřišská Tower has been open to the public since 2002. It is ten stories high and affords a magnificent view of the city. It has exhibition facilities, shops, a cafeteria and a restaurant where visitors can take a relaxing break.

Top, a detail of the Grand Hotel Europa, one of the finest examples of Art Nouveau architecture in Prague.

Centre, the church of Our Lady of the Snows, an important example of Gothic architecture.

The 66 metre high Jindřišská Tower, offers an opportunity to enjoy an extraordinary view of Prague.

Jubilee Synagogue
Jubilejní synagoga

The newest and also largest synagogue in Prague was designed by V. Stiasstný and A. Richter. Built during the early years of the 20th century it combines Art Nouveau influence with pseudo-Moorish ideas. The synagogue was name in honour of Franz Joseph I who celebrated the jubilee (50th anniversary) of his reign in 1898. The synagogue was built outside the old Jewish district and is still used for religious services.

A detail of the exterior of the Jubilee Synagogue that clearly shows Moorish influence.

The façade, of the synagogue an original blend of different styles, embellished with many decorative and religious elements such as – at the top – the tablets with the Ten Commandments, and the Hebrew verse from Psalm 118:20 'This is the gate of the Lord into which the righteous shall enter.'

The impressive interior of the National Museum of Prague and the elegant staircase.

Left, the interior of the Pantheon with a detail of the dome, and below some of the busts of the famous figures in Bohemian history, culture, science and statesmanship.

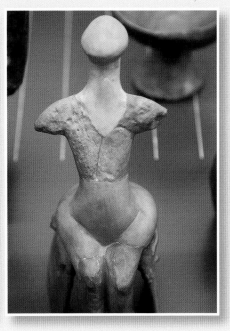

Bronze bull with iron inlays, from the Hallstatt civilization (6-5th cent. B.C.).

Celtic sculpture (2nd-1st cent. B.C.) from Mšecké Žehrovice (Bohemia).

Late Neolithic ceremonial figurine (latter half of the 5th millennium B.C.).

NATIONAL MUSEUM OF PRAGUE
Národní muzeum v Praze

This imposing neo-Renaissance building, which stands the full width of the southern end of *Václavské náměstí*, was built in the second half of the 19th century to a design by J. Schulz. It houses the main seat of the National Museum in Prague, with the **Museum of History and Natural History**, and the rooms used to house the **Library** (which numbers more than 1.3 million volumes and 8000 manuscripts). The domed **Pantheon** contains various busts and statues representing important figures from Czech culture. The Mineralogy, Botany, and Zoology collections are displayed in the side wings. The Historical and Archaeological sections contain some interesting coins, medals and theatrical exhibits. The National Museum also incorporates sections of the museums dedicated to *Ethnography, Musical Instruments, Náprstek* and *Physical Culture and Sport.* These are all housed in separate buildings.

Weights, knives with decorated hilts, iron implements, an oil lamp and a whetting stone, from Germanic settlements of the late Roman Era (3rd and 4th cent. A.D.).

A collection of swords and a belt from a tomb a Bučina, gold and silver plated brooches, necklaces and a bone comb from the Germanic civilization from the era of the migrations (5 and 6th cent. A.D.).

The National Theatre seen from the river.

The exhibition space created in the former basement storage rooms of the theatre in the 1980s. Here we can admire 21 stone slabs (and there may well be more) with inscriptions dating back to when the theatre was established.

NATIONAL THEATRE
Národní divadlo

This beautiful building, with its neo-Renaissance architectural features, stands on the right bank of the Vltava. It was erected in the second half of the 19th century to a design by J. Zítek. A short time after the staging of the very first performance the theatre was destroyed by fire and rebuilt in record time by J. Schulz, a follower of Zítek. Careful restoration work was carried out be- tween 1976 and 1983. The modern complex called the **New Stage** was added in 1983; this also includes the **Laterna Magica Theatre**. The northern **façade** is adorned with *Statues of Záboj and Lumír*, the work of artists from the workshop of A. Wagner. Two groups of statues adorn the attic storey, *Apollo and the Muses*, and *Goddesses of Victory*, both by B. Schnirch. *Allegories of Opera and*

Drama attributed to J. V. Myslbek stand above the side entrance, and the same artist also created the busts of illustrious figures. The **interior** of the National Theatre is richly decorated with paintings. The ceiling of the auditorium bears eight *Allegories representing the Arts* by F. Ženíšek who also painted the *Golden Age, Decline and Revival of Art,* which decorates the lobby on the first balcony.

The interior of the National Theatre; the ceiling is decorated with allegories of the arts.

The foyer of the first tier.

The elegant interior of the National Theatre, with the famous and quite magnificent curtain by V. Hynais in the background.

The "Dancing House" built between 1994 and 1996, is one of the symbols of the new Prague. Designed by the architects Frank O. Gehry and V. Milunič, it was inspired by the famous dancer, Fred Astaire and Ginger Rogers. Also known as "Ginger and Fred", it is an office building.

Charles Bridge

Karlův Most

The Charles Bridge is one of Prague's symbols *par excellence*. It joins the historic quarters of Staré Město and Malá Strana. Work was begun on its construction at the time of Charles IV (latter half of the 14th century) by P. Parléř and J. Ottl, and it was completed in the early 15th century, under the reign of Wenceslas IV. The strain of the centuries and the destructive floods of the Vltava have certainly put the Karlův Most to the test, and in fact two of its arches had to be rebuilt in 1890. The pedestrian bridge, which affords fantastic views of the city, is 516m long, 10m wide and is supported by 16 pillars. It is watched over by mighty towers at both ends, and the whole bridge was once part of the defensive works of Prague. Its monumental Gothic feel is softened and enlivened by what we might call a genuine open-air sculpture gallery: there are as many as 30 statues and groups of sculptures visible here, contributing to the magical atmosphere of Prague and the splendid views.

The Virgin Mary and Saint Bernard; M. V. Jäckel, 1709.

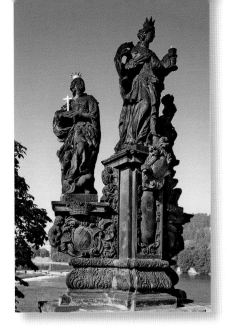

Saints Barbara, Margaret and Elizabeth;
F. M. Brokoff, 1707.

Left, two views of the Moldau, the
Charles Bridge and Starè Město.

Looking at Malá Strana from the
Charles Bridge in late evening.

In 1657, following the restoration of a bronze *Crucifix* which had stood here since the 14th century, statues and sculptural groups began to be placed along the parapet of the bridge: 26 of them between 1706 and 1714. Among the artists who have displayed their talents here are J. Brokofff and sons, M. B. Braun, and Josef and Emanuel Max. The group of *St Cyril and St Methodius* was sculpted in 1928 by K. Dvořák. Most of the statues have been replaced with copies since the originals are made of sandstone which is easily damaged by pollution. These are therefore kept in the *Lapidarium of the National Museum.* The *Statue of St Luitgard* is the most valuable, while the figure of *St Philip Benizzi* is the only work in marble. The only bronze statue is that of *St John of Nepomuk*, situated at the centre of the bridge. This is a 17th century work based on models by M. Rauchmüller and J. Brokofff. For luck, passers-by touch the engraved pedestal of the statue representing the saint as he was thrown into the river. On the parapet is a cross with five stars indicating the exact spot from which the saint was tossed to the waters. A Hebrew inscription near the *Calvary Group* commemorates the sacrilegious act of

Saint John of Nepomuk; J. Brokoff, 1683.

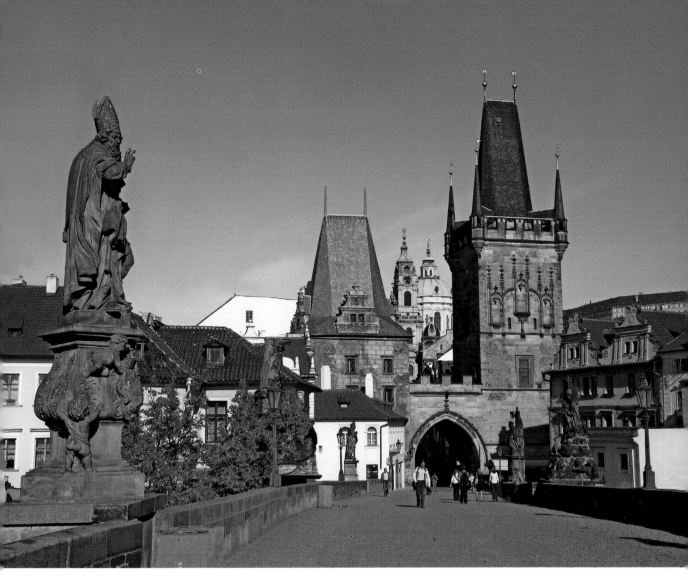

The Malá Strana Towers seen from the Charles Bridge.

A spectacular view of the Charles Bridge from the Starè Město Tower with the Malá Strana district and the Castle in the background.

*Saint Ludmilla;
M. B. Braun, 1720.*

a Jewish blasphemer (1696) which popular tradition has passed down to us. A scroll situated below the 19th century *Statue of St Francis Seraphicus* bears the verses of Psalm 90/11: "God will put his angels in charge of you to protect you wherever you go". Near the bridge (on Kampa Island) is the *Roland Column*, a 19th century copy of the 16th century original. The bridge is one of the focal points of tourist Prague: it is forever crowded with a babel of visitors, while artists, vendors and craftsmen offer their work for sale in an atmosphere reminiscent of the Parisian *Rive Gauche*. The **Towers of Malá Strana** mark the end of the bridge where it meets the quarter of the same name. The lower of the two towers, from the late 12th century, formed part of the old Judith Bridge. Some architectural and ornamental reconstruction work was carried out on it towards the end of the 16th century. The higher tower, built in the second half of the 15th century, was ordered by Jiří of Poděbrad and took the place of an old Romanesque tower.

Malá Strana
Little Quarter

The quarter of Malá Strana grew up, from around 1257, on the left bank of the Vltava, between the hills of Hradčany and Petřín. It was founded by Přemysl Otakar II whose intention it was to create a home for the German colonists. At the time of Charles IV the urban network underwent considerable expansion: old churches were restored or completed, and fortifications and defensive works appeared everywhere. During the 15th and 16th centuries the district was tormented by fires, as a result of which the building and extension work intensified, transforming Malá Strana into a coveted residential quarter. The area was chosen by the nobility and the wealthy for their permanent residences, and they enriched it with sumptuous palaces and magnificent churches. Malá Strana's charm was enhanced by the fact that the coronation processions of the Bohemian sovereigns passed through its streets.

View over the roofs of Malá Strana towards the church of St Nicholas.

NERUDOVA STREET
Nerudova ulice

This street, which branches off from *Malostranské náměstí* and climbs steeply up to the Castle, is one of the most characteristic and charming corners of the Malá Strana district. One of its main features is its wealth of elegant houses, some of the finest examples of late Baroque building in Prague. Characteristic coats of arms and shop signs, and picturesque front doors capture the visitor's attention: n° 12 was the home of the luthiers, the Edlingers, and the sign with three crossed violins is still here today; **Valkoun House**, at n° 14, was remodelled in late Baroque style by G. Santini; typical signs can also be seen on the houses named **The Golden Cup** (n° 16, Renaissance style), and

St John Nepomuk (n° 18, Baroque); the **Theatine Monastery** (n° 24) was the setting for performances of the *Kajetan Dramas* in Czech, while the adjacent building, **The Rocking Donkey**, provided the setting for a story by Neruda; n° 32 is the area's old pharmacy, restored in 1980 and now housing the **Museum of Pharmacy in Countries of the Bohemian Crown;** n° 33 is the **Bretfeld Palace**, also known as *Summer and Winter*; it was here that famous people such as Casanova and Mozart stayed; on the front door of the **House at the Golden Horseshoe** (n° 34) there is an image of *St Wenceslas*; at n° 49 a white swan forms the sign of an elegant Baroque residence. A nearby flight of steps leads to the Castle.

The original decorative details along the Nerudova Ulice: we can recognize some famous insignias such as At the Golden Chalice (top), At the Golden Horseshoe (right) and At the Three Violins (below).

Below, the house known as "of the three miners," an interesting building on the Nerudova ulice.

A lovely view of the Wallenstein Garden looking towards Sala Terrena.

The Main Hall: on the ceiling we can see the frescoed portrait of Wallenstein as the god Mars.

WALLENSTEIN PALACE
Valdštejnský palác

This magnificent residence, somewhere between a palace and a fortress, was built in the first half of the 17th century for the Bohemian commander Albrecht Wenzel Eusebius von Wallenstein. The plans were drawn up by A. Spezza and G. Pironi and the work was carried out by G. B. Marini. The building is a clear example of a residence commissioned by a layman who was antagonistic to royal power. Wallenstein wanted his actions and grandeur to be reflected in the majestic palace which was intended to overshadow the Castle with its size and majesty and this self-congratulatory intention is clear from the paintings which portray him.

The ceiling of the **Main Hall** bears a 17th century fresco (*Wallenstein in the Guise of Mars in his Triumphal Chariot*). The other rooms are decorated with paintings, including a *Portrait of Wallenstein on Horseback* in the **Knights' Hall**. The palace chapel's altar is said to be the oldest in the city. The building is also the seat of the Upper House. The **Wallenstein Garden** (*Valdštejnská zahrada*) is also part of the palace complex. It was modelled on the prototype of the Italian Baroque garden, and contains copies of sculptures by A. de Vries. The **Sala Terrena**, with frescoes by B. del Bianco, is used for theatrical and concert performances.

The fairytale-like Wallenstein Palace reflected in the pond that graces the stupendous gardens.

The Portrait of Wallenstein on Horseback, by Kristian Kaulfershov (1631) in the Knights' Hall.

Above, the Malá Fürstenberská Garden: this small pavilion is the point where the terrace of the lower garden meets the central staircase. On the ceiling, there is a rococo painting of a swing.

Top, the Velká Pálffyovská Garden: a detail of the parterre, in the foreground the ornamental pool with a statue of Triton, and in the background the portal crowned by an antique sundial.

The Palace Gardens
beneath the Castle
Palácové zahrady pod Pražským hradem

One of the most recent developments within the area of the gardens that lie to the south of the Castle, below what used to be a powerful system of defensive ramparts, involves the group of gardens collectively known as the **Palácové zahrady**, "Palace Gardens". In the 16th century pre-existing parklands and vineyards were transformed into splendid Italianate gardens and a century later, following their destruction by the occupying Swedish, the owners of the palaces overlooking the area had a new Baroque layout created, decorated with many statues, balustrades, terraces and fountains. In the late 20th century a sweeping initiative brought about the complete restoration of the old structures and has led to the rebirth of five of the old gardens: *Ledeburská*, *Malá Pálffyovská*, *Velká Pálffyovská*, *Kolowratská*, and *Malá Fürstenberská*. The first two were opened to the public in June 1995, the third in 1997 and the last two in 2000. Admired and supported by the European Union, the initiative has restored one of its most delightful features to the city of Prague.

*Ledeburská Garden: a beautiful staircase interrupted by Baroque
style terraces (designed by I. Palliardi) leads to the parterre
at the top of the garden and the octagonal temple.
In the background, the Prague Castle.*

*Malá Fürstenberská Garden: picturesque view
of the roofs of the Malý Fürstenberský Palace.*

The dome of the Church of Saint Nicholas in Malá Strana.

A view of the nave reveals the opulent decorations
and furnishings.

CHURCH OF ST NICHOLAS IN MALÁ STRANA

Chrám svatého Mikuláše

This splendid example of Bohemian Baroque architecture - previously belonging to the Jesuits who made it the focal point of the Counter Reformation in Bohemia - was built on the site of a Gothic church. Work on the building started at the beginning of the 18th century and lasted until 1756 when A. Lurago completed the Bell Tower (79m). The magnificent two-tier Baroque **façade** is decorated with the coats of arms of the Count of Kolovrat and S*tatues of the Fathers of the Church* carried out by followers of J. B. Kohl. The chancel and the high dome (79m) are the work of K. I. Dientzenhofer. The **interior** contains some magnificent Baroque ornaments, and the *ceiling* of the central nave was beautifully painted with frescoes by J. L. Kracker (18th century). These show *Episodes from the life of St Nicholas* and are some of the largest of their kind in Europe. The **dome** bears the splendid contemporary fresco (*Apotheosis of St Nicholas and Last Judgement*)

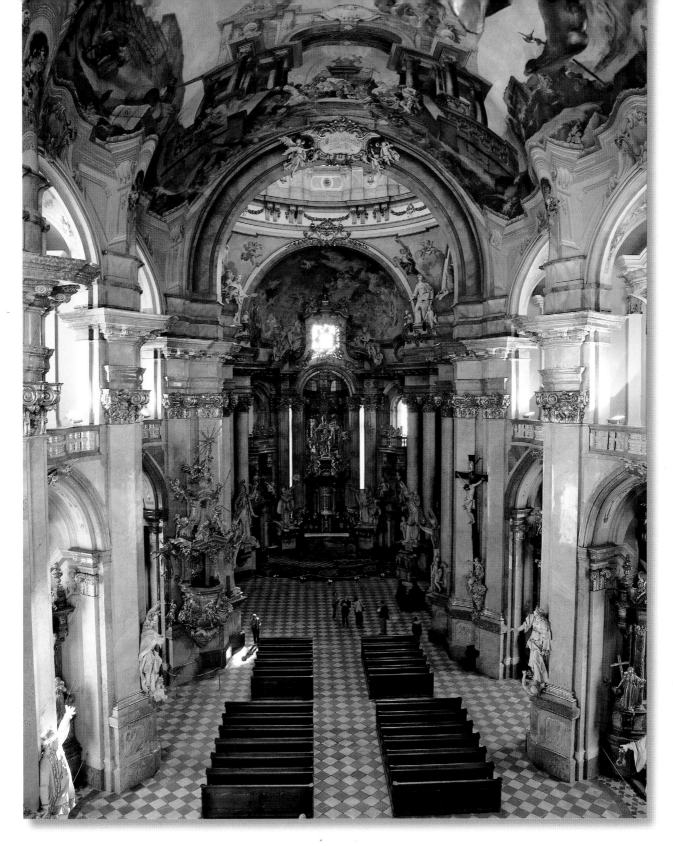

by F. X. Palko who is also responsible for the frescoes in the chancel, painted in collaboration with J. Hager. I. Platzer the Elder is the author of the sculptures situated in the central nave, the chancel and at the high altar (*St Nicholas*). Also note the 18th century *pulpit* by Richard and Peter Prachner, the grandiose, modern *organ* by T. Schwarz, as well as the altar-pieces and the paintings in the side chapels (works by J. L. Kracker, I. Raab, F. X. Palko, and F. Solimena). Beside the church is the former Baroque style *Jesuit College* which divides the square into two.

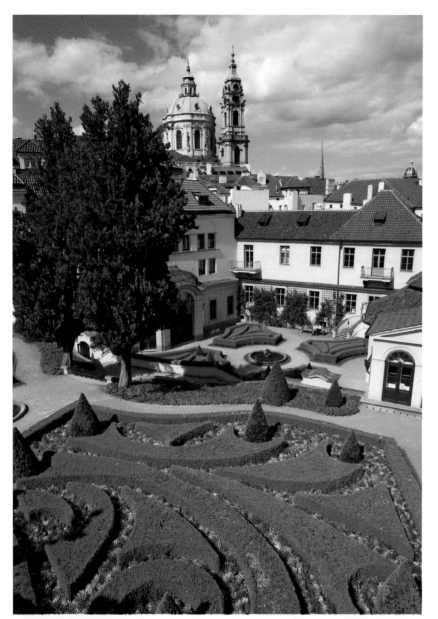

VRTBA PALACE
Vrtbovský palác

This building was renovated according to the canons of late Renaissance architecture in the first half of the 17th century. The **Garden** of the same name represents a fine example of a Baroque garden and is one of the most important in central Europe. It was designed by F. M. Kaňka, and built in the first half of the 18th century.

Of particular interest are the *statues of Ceres and Bacchus,* of the same period, by M. Braun, the double staircase with Baroque decorations and sculptures inspired by Greek mythology. A beautiful view can be enjoyed from the upper terrace.

A magnificent view of the upper terrace in the Vrtba Garden facing the Vrtba Palace and Malá Strana.

Below left, a view of the lower part of the garden with the Palace in the background; far right, adjacent to the Sala Terrena is the studio of the artist Mikoláš Aleš.

Below right, the interior of the Sala Terrena was magnificently frescoed by V.V. Reiner. On the front wall, Susanna and the Elders against a background of ancient ruins; Venus and Adonis decorate the ceiling, and on the sides are statues of Bacchus and Ceres by M.B. Braun.

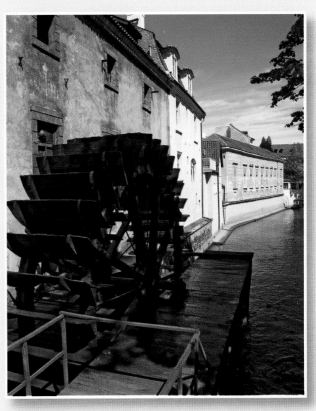

The steps that go from the Charles Bridge to the Kampa Island. Right, a picturesque view of Čertovka and the charming houses that line the street. In the foreground, an old millwheel.

KAMPA ISLAND

This island, mostly given over to parkland, lies between the two bridges, *Most Legií* and *Mánesův most*. The Čertovka (*Devil's Stream*), a branch of the Vltava which flows left from the main course of the river, separates Kampa Island from the picturesque quarter of Malá Strana. During Medieval times the waters of this branch of the Vltava fed several water mills. To the west the *Karlův Most* rests on the island, and looking south from the bridge along the *Čertovka* the wheel of an old mill can be seen; to the north the stream runs through the charming area known as the 'Venice of Prague', with its characteristic canal and picturesque houses.

A detail of the "John Lennon Wall": after the singer was killed this wall was covered with words inspired by him and his songs, and become a symbol of freedom and peace for the young people of Prague. In spite of the regime's opposition, the site survived and is now a popular tourist destination. This image was painted after 1989.

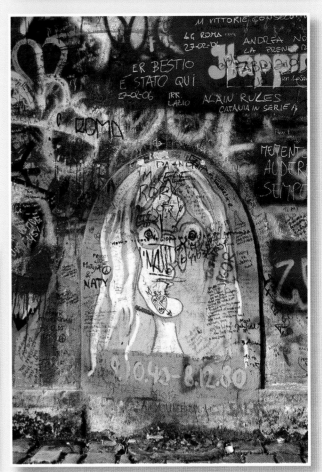

The Kampa Museum of Contemporary Art is housed in an old mill.

The Petřín Tower soars over the eponymous hill; below the Church of Saint Lawrence seen from the tower.

MIRROR MAZE
Bludiště

The maze is housed in an attractive pavilion which also contains a wooden model of the Charles Gate, and a diorama of *The Defence of Prague against the Swedes in 1648*. The painting is by A. Liebscher and V. Bartoněk (late 19th century). The Mirror Maze was built at the same time as the Observation Tower and is one of the attractions of Petřín Hill.

OBSERVATORY
Hvězdárna

The observatory houses the **Czech Academy of Science Astronomical Institute**. Part of the building was opened to the public for the first time in 1928. Guided tours and astronomical events are organised for those interested in this subject. The collection of telescopes used for observations ranges from modern instruments to models now obsolete.

CHURCH
OF ST LAWRENCE
Kostel svatého Vavřince

The present Baroque appearance of this place of worship dates back to the 18th century when an earlier Romanesque building, first recorded in the mid-12th century, was reconstructed by I. Palliardi. The **façade** is enhanced with a 19th century *Statue of St Adalbert*, the work of F. Dvořáček. Inside the church note the late 17th century painting above the high altar showing *The Torment of St Adalbert*, by J. C. Monnos. The Sacristy ceiling is decorated with an 18th century fresco illustrating *The Legend of the Foundation of the Church of St Adalbert*.

PETŘÍN
OBSERVATION TOWER
Petřínská rozhledna

The fact that Prague is often defined as the 'Paris of the East' by travel publications is only partly due to the pleasant nature of its monuments and localities; the term also derives from this iron tower which was built for the Prague Industrial Exhibition in 1891 as an imitation of the Parisian Eiffel Tower. It is 62.5m tall and in the past was used as a television tower. Still used to reach Petřín, a funicular railway was made to transport visitors from the exhibition to the tower. Unlike its French counterpart, the climb to the top had to be made on foot (299 steps), but the view is well worth the effort: on a clear day the 'Golden City', its hills and the surrounding areas are all visible. A lift to the top is now available to carry visitors and the disabled to the top.

The Castle

Pražský hrad

No longer encumbered by its original function as a purely defensive stronghold, today Prague Castle is more like a small town presenting a harmonious appearance, as the various separate components have been quite elegantly unified. The residence of the dukes of Bohemia was situated on this hill as early as the 980s when prince Bořivoj founded the first royal palace here. According to legend, princess Libuše originally foresaw its foundation in a prophetic vision and predicted that a rich and powerful city would arise on this green slope on the river Vltava. It is also said that an ancient Slav place of worship was located here. In any case, St Mary's Church was built here at the end of the 9th century and in about 920 duke Vratislav I also built the church dedicated to St George and consecrated in 925. Not long after, the Rotunda of St Vitus was built by Wenceslas, who would subsequently be assassinated and then too join the glorious ranks of the saints. In the 10th century the Castle was more or less exactly the same size as that of today and an early wooden fortification probably also existed. Frequently besieged and destroyed and just as frequently rebuilt and fortified, the Castle experienced a long period of energetic development from the 12th century when the Přemyslid princes took up residence there. Under Přemysl Otakar I, Wenceslas I and Přemysl Otakar II, despite long periods of war and threats of invasion, the Castle buildings increased and included the Royal Palace, the Romanesque part of which was begun by Soběslav I in the first half of the 12th century; enlarged and modernised in 1252 by the future Otakar II, it was entirely destroyed by a storm in 1280. Under Wenceslas II and his son Wenceslas III, repair and restoration work was only slowly undertaken. An unfortunate period followed under John of Luxembourg and the Castle was neglected, but during the mid 14th century, his son, Charles IV, who had been educated at the court of France, built a new Royal Palace and Cathedral worthy of the newly flourishing city, thus bringing a sophisticated and previously unknown splendour to the Castle. In turn his son, Wenceslas IV, continued and extended his father's achievements. A series of rulers followed who were more interested in wars than in improving the capital of the kingdom until finally Vladislav II Jagellonsky turned his attention to the Castle at the start of the 16th century. He was responsible for the new fortifications but also for a series of new buildings

View of the Charles Bridge, Malá Strana and the majestic Prague Castle.

and plans. With the arrival of Ferdinand I, a member of the Hapsburg family (1526-1564), it was decided that the Castle required a new look and character, more suited to the requirements of an important court: gardens were created, buildings were enlarged and its magnificence increased. The devastating fire of 1541 made radical rebuilding urgent and also facilitated the work of improvement and development instigated by first Maximilian II and then Rudolph II (an art lover and enthusiast of the sciences), who enriched the Castle with both his numerous collections and his illustrious scholarly guests, such as Tycho de Brahe and Kepler. In the early 17th century under Ferdinand II the Baroque was splendidly introduced to the Castle and its gardens. The style continued to develop under Ferdinand III, Leopold I (who laid the first stone of the Cathedral's Baroque completion in 1673) and Charles VI. Finally, in the mid 18th century, Maria Theresa of Austria commissioned the court architect, Nicola Pacassi, to plan and carry out the definitive appearance and arrangement of the general structure. The Castle then fell into a kind of oblivion, only interrupted by sporadic and sumptuous coronation ceremonies. Impoverished by expropriations and damaged by extensive military use of its buildings, it came to life once more under Ferdinand V who chose it as his personal residence, and its role was once again reasserted in the 20th century when the Republic came into being. The Castle was chosen as the natural residence for the President and was restored and adapted for its new purpose by Josip Plečnik. More recently Václav Havel initiated the restoration of many rooms and areas that had for long been neglected and inaccessible; returned once more to their original splendour, these are now open to the public.

A glimpse of the city dominated by the majestic Castle.

The main entrance to the Castle from the Hradčanské náměstí.

Opposite page, the Giants' Gate.

Giants' Gate

Clearly Hapsburg in style, the name of the gate is derived from the *gigantic figures* which dominate the pillars at the entrance, designed by I. Platzer the Elder and made between 1770 and 1771. All along the railings on either side of the gate, are more statues portraying cherubs, an eagle, (a symbol of the Hapsburg rulers), and a lion (animal symbolizing the kingdom of Bohemia), forming a varied series of contemporary works, also by Ignác Platzer. The figures seen here today are copies however, as the originals, made of sandstone that is badly affected by climatic conditions, were removed and replaced at the beginning of the 20th century.

FIRST COURTYARD

The Castle Gate leads into the Ceremonial Courtyard (or First Courtyard). This is located where once there was a deep ravine dividing the district of Hradčany from the older buildings of the Castle, and only crossed by bridges.

This court was also built during the Hapsburg period (1763-1771) when Maria Theresa of Austria instructed the court architect Nicola Picassi, assisted by the master builder A. Lurago, to design this great square where the pre-existing gully had been filled in. To give the square an elegant appearance the architect created three fine buildings in the Viennese style, forming a majestic U shape.

Thus the concept of the defensive fortress was clearly abandoned and the appearance of the Castle began to evolve into that of an airy imperial residence. This continued with the construction of the New Palace which would later be extended with the addition of the buildings that surround the Second Courtyard. The halls, apartments and rooms of the **North** and **South Wings** are still used for state visits, while the **West Wing** is generally used for official receptions and events.

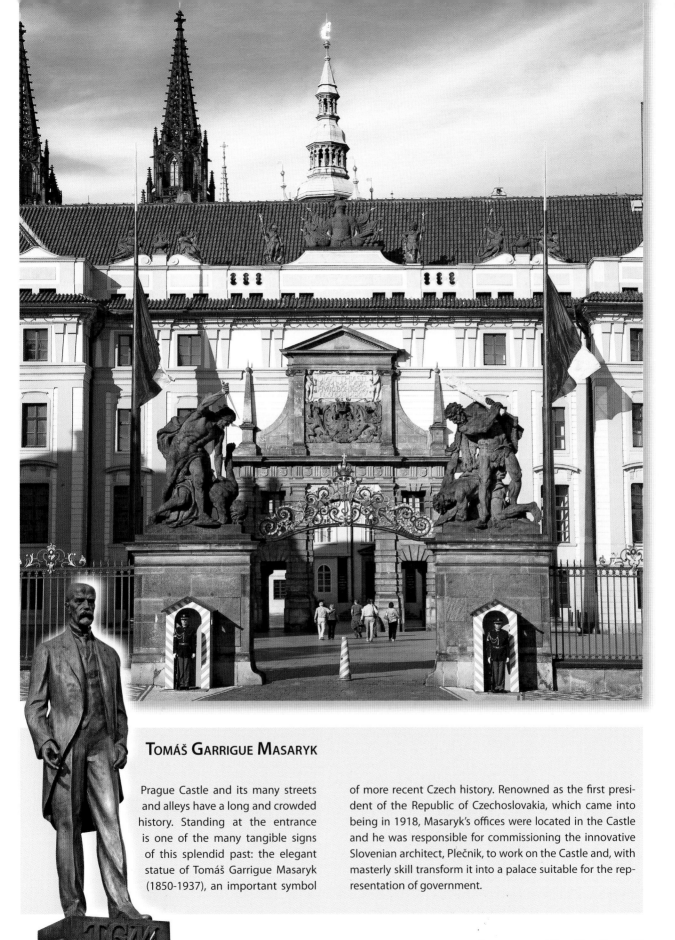

Tomáš Garrigue Masaryk

Prague Castle and its many streets and alleys have a long and crowded history. Standing at the entrance is one of the many tangible signs of this splendid past: the elegant statue of Tomáš Garrigue Masaryk (1850-1937), an important symbol of more recent Czech history. Renowned as the first president of the Republic of Czechoslovakia, which came into being in 1918, Masaryk's offices were located in the Castle and he was responsible for commissioning the innovative Slovenian architect, Plečnik, to work on the Castle and, with masterly skill transform it into a palace suitable for the representation of government.

Matthias' Gate

Preceded by two lofty flag staffs 25 metres high, originally made from the trunk of a single fir tree from Moravia, wedged between the buildings of the West Wing the 17th-century Matthias' Gate leads to the Second Courtyard. Like a solitary triumphal arch, it was erected by Matthias II in 1614 (and is therefore much earlier than the buildings that surround it) in early Baroque style though with Rudolphesque influences, it was probably the work of the court architect, Giovanni Maria Filippi, though it has also been suggested that the design was by Scamozzi. It is clearly a commemorative structure: engraved at the top are the titles and heraldic emblem of Emperor Matthias, while below, beneath the cornice, are the numerous coats of arms of the countries in his domain. Access to the various rooms of the splendid West Wing is from here, via the two stairways that lead out of the entrance way.

The sandstone Matthias Gate once stood alone, like a triumphal arch.

THE CHANGING OF THE GUARD

For centuries a small group of guards has protected the safety of the castle. Though today they wear elegant modern uniforms newly designed in 1989 by Theodor Pištěk, life was rather more difficult in the past in particular in the 18th century when, only paid with free lodging and wood for their fires for warmth, they were reduced to only 24 men armed with barely three bullets

each. The institution of the castle guards survived, however, and even now every day on the hour from 5 in the morning until 11 pm the changing of the guard is performed in front of the gates. The most spectacular of these ceremonies however, takes place at midday under the eyes of an admiring public, complete with brass fanfares and the exchange of flags.

NORTH WING: RUDOLPH GALLERY AND SPANISH HALL

An enthusiastic collector, principally of works of art and especially paintings, Emperor Rudolph II created a vast and rare collection and commissioned G. Gargiolli to design the most suitable setting possible for it in the stable block - the splendid **Rudolph Gallery**. As time passed, however, the prestigious imperial collection seemed destined to be dismantled. However, today's gallery, opened in 1965, is still based on the original nucleus of precisely the imperial collections of Rudolph and boasts masterpieces by Paolo Veronese, Rubens, Titian and Tintoretto, flanked by more re-

cent paintings from the 18th, 19th and 20th centuries by artists of Prague. Just as interesting, and designed by G. M. Filippi, is the enormous **Spanish Hall**, originally built between 1602 and 1606, but refurbished several times in the 18th and 19th centuries giving it the clearly Baroque appearance remaining today. Also furnished to house the collections of the emperor, it gradually assumed a purely formal role hosting court celebrations and balls.

Shots of the magnificent Spanish Gallery, one of the most important in the entire Castle and, above, the adjacent Gallery of Rudolph II.

Left, a detail of the outside of the Chapel of the Holy Cross and, right, the lavish interior.

Chapel of the Holy Cross

In the south-east area of the Second Courtyard is the simple and elegant Chapel of the Holy Cross, built by A. Lurago between 1758 and 1763 according to a design by Nicola Pacassi. However, all that remains of that period are the high altar made by Ignác Platzer and a *Crucifix* painted by S. Balko.
All the rest of the building dates from the 19th century restoration, resulting from the need to adapt the building to its role as a private chapel for the emperor.

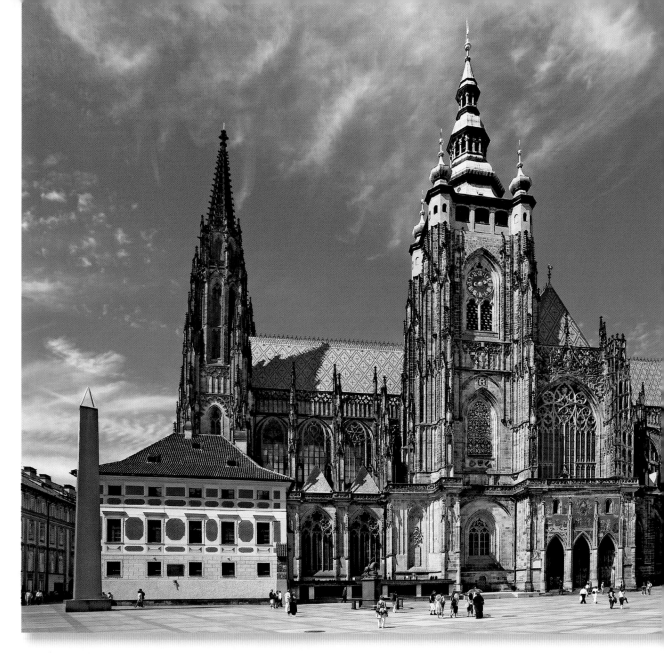

*The elegant Third Courtyard with the Old Provost's House,
the Cathedral of St Vitus and a wing of the Royal Palace.*

A night time view of the Cathedral of St Vitus.

*View of the Third Courtyard, with the statue
of St George facing the entrance to the Royal Palace.*

The equestrian statue of Saint George, patron of soldiers and knights. This is a copy of the fourteenth century bronze statue that now stands inside the Royal Palace.

THIRD COURTYARD

An entrance set into the Central wing, where robust remains of the Romanesque fortifications can still be seen, leads into the heart of the Castle, the large third courtyard, originally on two levels that were merged during the 20th century by the spectacular paving in granite by Plečnik. Modern and old features mingle harmoniously in this area, with the Cathedral towering above. Archaeological excavations have for long investigated the historical and architectural history of the original nucleus of the Castle here. The **Old Provost's House**, built on the site of the Romanesque Bishop's palace of which an original window survives, is flanked by a many modern and linear granite **monoliths**.

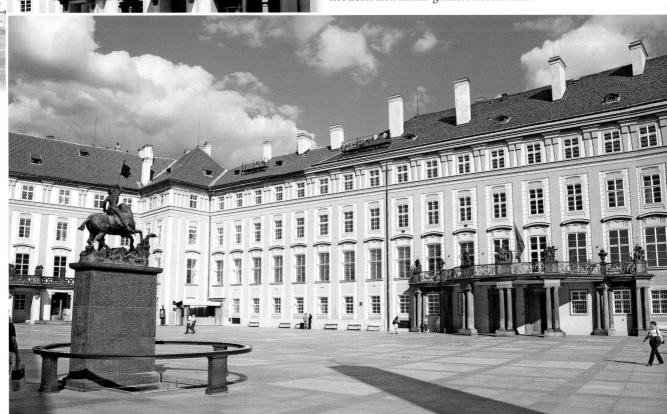

CATHEDRAL OF ST VITUS
Chrám sv. Víta

The history of Prague Cathedral, the true spiritual centre of the entire country, is lengthy and complex. In 925, where this impressive monument now stands, St Wenceslas built the small circular Romanesque structure of St Vitus, his future burial place, flanked not long afterwards by the bishops' residence and subsequently replaced in 1060 by a new basilica with three naves and two choirs. It was not until 1344 that Charles IV commissioned the French architect, Mathieu d'Arras, to build a new Gothic cathedral for the rapidly growing city, which had recently become an archbishopric – a cathedral that would be worthy of housing the body of such a great sovereign as St Wenceslas, the country's patron. The foundation stone was laid on 21 November of that year and the great French cathedrals provided the model for the construction. When Mathieu d'Arras died the work was continued, under the guidance and direct control of Charles IV, by the Swabian architect and sculptor, Petr Parléř, one of the fathers of European Gothic, until his death in 1399. His sons, Jan and Wenceslas, took over but work was interrupted in the 1420s by the Hussite wars. At the time, most of the bell tower had been built but not even half of the building was completed, and the choir was closed with a wall forming a kind of temporary façade so that religious services could be held. The ambulatory and a first Renaissance dome were built in the second half of the 16th century. Thus the Cathedral remained unfinished, with a truncated appearance – the nave barely begun beyond the transept. A series of disastrous events then followed: in 1541 there was a dreadful fire, in 1620 it was pillaged by the Calvinists, a century later it was severely attacked and damaged by the Prussians, and in 1760 lightning struck causing another fire as well as destroying the only existing tower at the time. The work of building the west nave did not then begin until 1872 when Joseph Mocker's project continued the work in complete harmony with the monumental style already existing. When Mocker died, Kamil Hilbert took over in 1899 and in 1929, one thousand years after the death of St Wenceslas, the Cathedral, with its imperious stature and interwoven buttresses so characteristic of the most perfect Gothic architecture, could finally be said to be finished.

The splendid apse, decorated with spires and pinnacles, is illuminated by stained glass windows and surrounded by chapels in the French Gothic style.

The awe-inspiring main façade of the Cathedral of St Vitus.

The lofty central nave of the Cathedral, enhanced with unusual interlacing in the vault, the glowing rose window, and the brightly coloured stained glass windows in the apse.

The interior

Some 124 metres long, just over 33 high, 60 metres at the widest point of the transept, with two lower naves flanking the central one, the interior of St Vitus' Cathedral is austere, unadorned and harmonious. Light filters through the large stained glass windows and below these, with a height of about 14 metres, runs an elegant and original ambulatory, known as the **internal triforium or arcade**, decorated with a magnificent gallery of sculptures. Below is a long sequence of **chapels**, some of which are antique and were designed by Mathieu d'Arras and Petr Parléř, some of which are more recent. Overhead is the spectacular, uninterrupted interlacing of the meshed pattern in the **vaults**, a genuine innovation in 14th century Europe and once more created by the genius of Petr Parléř. On the west side is the kaleidoscopic colour effect of the **stained glass window**;

27,000 pieces of coloured glass form scenes from the *Creation*. Occupying the centre of the nave is the *burial place of St Adalbert*, for whom a chapel was first built on the exterior of the provisional west façade of the unfinished Cathedral, though this was later destroyed when building work began once more. On the east side is the transept which crosses the nave more or less at the point where building of the Cathedral was interrupted in the 15th century. Standing guard at the majestic intersection of nave and transept are eight wooden statues of the patron saints of Bohemia: Adalbert, John of Nepomuk, Ludmilla, Norbert, Procopius, Sigismund, Wenceslas and Vitus.

The north part of the transept ends in a magnificent Renaissance tribune which was originally used as a monumental and temporary closure for the choir in the unfinished

Above and right, the splendid modern stained glass windows by Alfons Muchas (1860-1939) universally acknowledged as one of the greatest masters of the Art Nouveau style. Below, details of some of the other magnificent stained glass windows that embellish the cathedral.

Cathedral (it was transferred here in 1924), now finished with an 18th-century organ. The south end is lit by a glistening neo-Gothic *stained glass window*, the panes of which represent scenes from the *Universal Judgment*, made in 1939 by Max Švabinský. Lit by three large windows of 20th-century stained glass is the grand *apse*, preceded by the impressive **royal mausoleum** made by the Hapsburgs at the end of the 16th century, where the reclining figures of Ferdinand I, his

The elegant Chapel of St Sigismund designed by Petr Parléř contains the remains of Sigismund, king of the Burgundians Bohemia.

The tomb of St Vitus with the nineteenth century sandstone statue by Emanuel Max.

wife, Anna Jagellonsky and their son, Maximilian II are visible behind the statue of the *Risen Christ*. Made by Alexander Collin between 1570 and 1589, this grandiose marble monument is a magnificent conclusion to the **royal crypt** below. Reached from the Chapel of the Holy Cross and rebuilt in the first half of the 20th century, various members of the imperial family have been interred here, behind an elegant enclosure, since the late 16th century.

One of the wooden relief carvings behind the choir stalls; this one depicts the Flight of Frederick the Elector Palatine from Prague; the carving, by Gaspare Becheteler antedates 1630.

The Chapels

There are some 19 chapels in the Cathedral, from the nave to the apse and the south tower. All are splendid and some more grandiose than others. The **Chapel of St Sigismund** is an architectural work by Petr Parléř. The **Chapel of St John the Baptist**, originally an old structure but rebuilt in the 19th century,

The statue of Cardinal Bedřich Schwarzenberg, archbishop of Prague (1892-1895), by J. V. Myslbek, stands in front of the Pernštejn Chapel.

The magnificent silver funerary monument to Saint John of Nepomuk by J. E. Fischer von Erlach (1733-1737), is framed by an elegant baldachin and dominated by the figure of the kneeling saint holding a crucifix.

houses the Gothic tombs of princes Bořivoj II and Boleslav II as well as the 16th century tombs of archbishops Antonín Brusa of Mohelnice and Martin Medek. The **Chapel of the Virgin Mary** was commissioned to be built by Charles IV on the spot where the foundation stone of the Cathedral was laid, and is opposite the *tomb of St Vitus*. Among the oldest in Europe, in the **Chapel of the Holy Reliquaries** are the magnificent sepulchres of Přemysl Otakar I and Přemysl Otakar II, whose burial crown, imperial orb and sceptre have been discovered. But the most beautiful, famous and frequently visited is without doubt the **Chapel of St Wenceslas**, on the east side of the south tower, corresponding to the apse of the old Romanesque rotunda, commissioned by Charles IV and built by Petr Parléř who completed it in 1367.

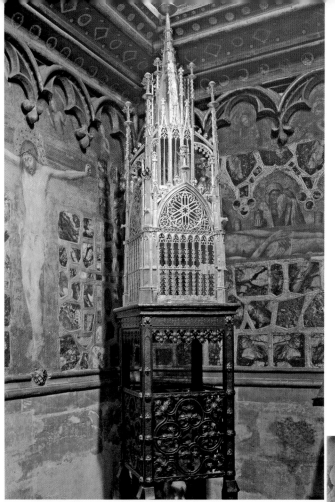

Chapel of St Wenceslas

The Chapel has a square plan, is larger in size than the other chapels and is also more sophisticated with almost 1,350 semi-precious stones set into the walls creating a grandiose frame for the fresco cycle dedicated to the *Passion of Christ* (1372-1373). This chapel is, moreover, the most sacred as it houses the relics of prince Wenceslas, patron saint of Bohemia, on the same spot where they were originally buried, in what was then the St Vitus rotunda.

A fine door leads to the stairway up to the Crown Room. Higher up, the chapel has a second fresco cycle, dated 16th-17th century and representing scenes from the life of St Wenceslas. The chapel also contains an unusual tower-shaped reliquary and an excellent painted stone statue of the saint (1373), probably by a nephew of Petr Parléř, standing against the background of another fresco with angels and saints.

The Chapel of Saint Wenceslas with its fine frescoes, and above a detail showing the tabernacle.

The exterior of the Vladislav Hall, the stronghold of the old Royal Palace.

The majestic Vladislav Hall.

THE ROYAL PALACE
Královský palác

From the Royal Oratory of the Cathedral a covered passage leads directly to the old Royal Palace, on the south side of the Third Courtyard. The building came into being in the 12th century when prince Soběslav I had the first royal residence built here in Romanesque style and with a rectangular plan. The massive south walls of the palace also became part of the Castle defences. In 1185 the Chapel of All Saints was constructed alongside and in the middle of the 13th century, Přemysl Otakar II had the palace enlarged. It was not until the 14th century when Charles IV was still only the hereditary prince, that the building was significantly enlarged towards the north and the west, thus acquiring space to create the large reception rooms, and the Gothic style was supplanted by the Romanesque. When Wenceslas IV in turn decided that rebuilding was required, he intended to transform the palace into a comfortable and elegant residence for the royal family, though he also extended the buildings and modified the direct passage between the palace and Chapel of All Saints. Due to the Hussite wars the palace was for long abandoned and it was king Vladislav Jagellonsky who restored it to its regal function and status, financing a series of impressive building projects involving in particular the first floor and especially the creation of the attractive **Vladislav Hall**. After the disastrous fire of 1541 it was Ferdinand I of Hapsburg who had to tackle the problem of the serious damage caused, at the same time rebuilding the **Hall of the Diets**. As time passed, however, the palace gradually ceased to be used for its original function, first losing its role as a residence for the royal family (the Hapsburgs in fact preferred the rooms in the western part of the castle) while the administrative function was greatly reduced, though it continued to fulfil a role as the setting for important public ceremonies. Lastly, as part of the project for radically rebuilding the entire castle carried out in the 18th century by Nicola Pacassi and commissioned by Empress Maria Theresa, the façades were all modified to achieve an appearance in complete harmony with the surrounding buildings and the old Royal Palace was thus definitively integrated with the new Hapsburg image of this imposing complex.

The façade of the Basilica of Saint George.

ST GEORGE'S MONASTERY AND BASILICA
Klášter sv. Jiří - Bazilika sv. Jiří

St George's was originally the main square in the Castle and, before the building of the Cathedral, was much larger than today. Prince Vratislav I had a single nave church built here in 920, consecrated in 925 and destined to house the remains of the first Czech martyr, his mother princess Ludmilla, who was canonised shortly after and was also the grandmother of another, future saint, Wenceslas the son of Vratislav. In 973 Boleslaus II and his sister, the abbess Mlada, built the neighbouring monastery and it consequently became necessary to enlarge this little church transforming it into a basilica with three naves, three apses to the east and two crypts. In the years to come the Přemyslid sovereigns were to be buried here, signifying the importance this religious building had now acquired. Seriously damaged during the siege of 1142, the church was rebuilt quite a bit longer, and with

two **towers**, the more northerly one of which would be integrated into the cloister during the Baroque period, while the more southerly one was probably built on the spot where the Chapel of the Virgin Mary had stood in the past, probably over the site of the original burial place of St Ludmilla. The **chapel** built to house the remains of the saint dates from the 13th century and is located on the south side of the Romanesque apse (the stone *sepulchre* is instead a 14th century work by Petr Parléř, commissioned by Charles IV). A new *west façade* was made during the 14th century, also by Petr Parléř. It was remodelled with red brickwork in Baroque style in the 17th century and in the same century the **Chapel of St John of Nepomuk** was made in the south west corner of the basilica and decorated with a stupendous Baroque *fresco* in the cupola representing the *Apotheosis of St John of Nepomuk*, by Václav Reiner. The *south façade* is also interesting with a Romanesque wall that encloses a Renaissance doorway leading to the south nave and dated 1515, a magnificent creation by Benedikt Ried. Originally entrusted to the Benedictine nuns for the education of young daughters of the Bohemian aristocracy, the evolution of the monastery was similar to that of the church. It was also badly damaged during the siege of 1142 but was quickly rebuilt larger and with an additional storey. Helped by the fact that its abbesses usually belonged to aristocratic families, if not indeed the royal family, the convent quickly grew in size and importance, with the addition of a large Gothic cloister, while the abbesses acquired the right and privilege of crowning the queen of Bohemia. Destroyed by the fire of 1541, rebuilt in Renaissance style, completely restructured a century later according to the new dictates of the Baroque style, including an entirely new **cloister** which replaced the older Gothic one altogether, this powerful monastery was suppressed in 1782 by Joseph II and the building was transformed into a barracks. Despite the Baroque façade, the interior of the church still has an austere Romanesque appearance with lofty women's galleries, *funerary monuments* marking the sepulchres of the Přemyslid princes, including the sepulchre of the church's founder, Vratislav I, fine *frescoes* in the conches of the apses and chapels, and a *crypt* with 12th-century cross vaults. Since 1975, on the first floor the monastery has housed the **section of the National Gallery in Prague** dedicated to the Mannerist paintings belonging to the court of Rudolph II as well as Bohemian Baroque works of the 17th and 18th centuries, with works of art by H. Von Aachen, Spranger, A. De Vries, P. Brandl, V. V. Reiner and M. B. Braun.

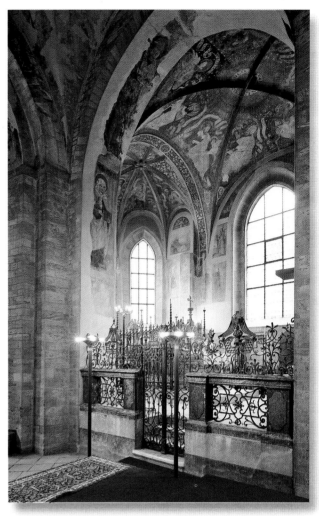

The chapel where the remains of Saint Ludmilla are conserved, and below, a view of the nave.

GOLDEN LANE
Zlatá ulička

Running in a west to east direction behind St George's Monastery, this picturesque and romantic little street, also known as Alchemists' Lane, is an obligatory port of call for visitors to the Castle and represents the tradition of Prague as a "magical city". In dark and smoky laboratories here Rudolph II's alchemists sought to reveal the myths of the philosopher's stone and the production of gold. The tale is one of the most intriguing to have developed about the city and its Castle. The reality is that the Renaissance houses along this lane were built in the second half of the 16th century to replace twenty or so temporary and ramshackle houses that had sprung up here set against the Castle walls, incorporating the remains of the medieval fortifications to the south and replacing the older defensive terraces to the north, in order to provide lodgings for Rudolph II's servants and guards. It was later that the goldsmiths also moved into this area. Many centuries later, between 1916 and 1917, at number 22 of the Lane, Franz Kafka wrote some of his short stories. Today the little houses that once were crafts-

Views of the colourful and picturesque cottages in the Golden Lane.

*A panoramic view of Prague
from Malá Strana.*

*One of the splendid interiors
of Lobkowicz Palace.*

men's' workshops and dwellings for the poor, are attractive
shops where souvenirs and artistic and crafts items can be
bought. A quite delightful view can be enjoyed from the
castle walls behind, where a long *defensive corridor* winds
its way along the top of the houses, still providing a con-
nection between the late Gothic terraces of the fortifications and the Castle itself.

LOBKOWICZ PALACE
Lobkowiczský palác

Opposite the Burgrave's House stands an impressive
building structured around two courtyards. The
Lobokowicz Palace was the residence of the powerful
Pernštejn family during the 16th century and in 1627 after being extended, it passed to the owners for whom it
is now named. Between 1651 and 1668 the Lobkowicz
family had the buildings entirely restructured by Carlo
Lurago in Baroque style. Some of the rooms on the first
floor, such as the two halls and nearby chapel, are still in
their original state, while the rest of the palace houses
the **section of the National Museum** dedicated to the
ancient history of Bohemia.

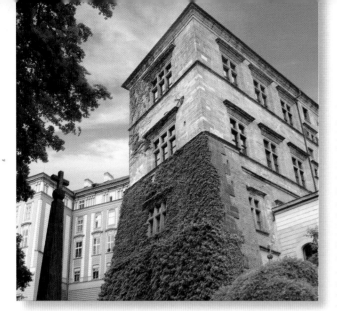

CASTLE GARDENS
Zahrady Pražského hradu

Once the Castle no longer needed to fulfil a function as a purely defensive stronghold, and it had become possible to emphasize its role as a noble residence used for purposes of representation, it was finally possible to develop its more pleasant and enjoyable aspects. Thus, around the perimeter of the fortifications delightful gardens came into being and thrived. It was the Hapsburg sovereign, Ferdinand I, who oversaw their creation in 1534, but their present splendid appearance, enhanced by the presence of numerous Renaissance and Baroque statues, is thanks to the 20th century architect Josip Plečnik who began their reorganization after 1918, an arduous task that is not entirely completed even today.

South Gardens

The **South Gardens** on the southern side of the Castle are quite delightful; they are connected to the Third Courtyard by the *Bull Staircase* and consist of the **Garden on the Ramparts** (*Zahrada Na Valech*) and the **Paradise Garden** (*Rajská zahrada*) which were already well developed in the 16th century, but redesigned and improved during the 20th century by Plečnik. In the shade of the dramatic and majestic south façade of the Castle, skilfully rearranged by Pacassi, the gardens are a series of incredible botanical features, historical ruins and artistic masterpieces. The **Bellevue Pavilion** was made by Plečnik in 1924 with faintly Egyptian overtones and a splendid viewpoint. There is also an **Alpine Flower Garden**, the **Hartig Garden**, which only became part of the South Gardens in 1965, the **Matthias Pavilion**, a cylindrical structure made in 1617 for Emperor Matthias, as well as two little stone monuments close by the Ludvík Wing commemorating the spot where two of the unfortunate victims of the Prague Defenestration fell. Seen from this elegant green paradise, even the Castle seems to assume a sweeter and softer appearance. And from here we return to the Castle, to the west entrance standing at the end of the route through the South Gardens.

Above, a glimpse of the Ludwig Wing, scene of the Defenestration of Prague.

Below, the Noblewomen's Institute seen from the Garden on the Ramparts (Zahrada Na Valech).

Above, the Queen Anne's Summer Palace.

Below, one of the beautiful statues decorating the Real Tennis Pavilion and the cathedral seen from the gardens of the Riding School.

Royal Gardens

Along the fortifications on the north is the crevice of a deep gulley with a stream which, once its obvious use as a defensive feature became superfluous, fell into disuse and was been substantially abandoned, evolving into a pleasant shelter for many animals, including deer. There are no longer any deer, but their presence in the past is still clearly evoked by the name of the **Deer Moat**. The **Powder Bridge** crosses it in the area of the old 17th century **Stables** and **Riding School** as well as the famous **Lions' Court**. At the back of this courtyard lie the splendid **Royal Gardens**, for centuries famous for their tropical plants, the exotic fruits that could be gathered there, and the fertile vegetable gardens. Moreover, it was here that certain bulbs imported from Istanbul were cultivated and the tulips that bloomed were then imported by Holland. It was precisely to provide easier access to this magnificent corner of the gardens that the Powder Bridge was built in the mid 16th century. The pretty pathways are enhanced by various elegant buildings, such as the large **Real Tennis Pavilion** (the oldest stone building of its kind in Europe, it was built in 1569 by Wohlmut) and the **Orangery**, originally 16th century, but attractively renovated in the 20th century. Also known as the Belvedere for its wonderful view, the **Summer Palace of Queen Anne** is at the end, beyond the small garden; built by Ferdinand I for his wife, Anne Jagellonsky between 1535 and 1563, it has an unusual roof shaped like the keel of a boat and is surrounded by delightful airy arches. It is difficult to imagine that this pretty, delicate building was destined to be used as a barracks and army workshop for almost a century between the 1700s and 1800s.

Hradčany

The stern statue of Masaryk looks down on Hradčany Square, while street musicians entertain the tourists and passers-by.

Elegant architecture defines the Archbishop's Palace.

The sgraffito decorations on the façade of the Schwarzenberg Palace create the illusion of diamond-point rustication.

HRADČANY SQUARE
Hradčanské náměstí

This charming square, given a certain dignity by the Baroque buildings which overlook it, has always formed the entrance to the Castle. It is adorned with the 18th century *Plague Column* (F. M. Brokoff). The surrounding buildings are the result of reconstruction carried out after the fire of 1541.

ARCHBISHOP'S PALACE
Arcibiskupský palác

The original building was a Renaissance residence which was then transformed in the second half of the 16th century, extended around 1600 and converted to Baroque style in the second half of the 17th century. In the same period the architect J. B. Mathey, who had designed the Baroque transformations, completed the splendid main portal. In the second half of the 18th century J. J. Wirch gave the palace's **façade** its present day Rococo appearance. Above the coat of arms of the Prince-Archbishop A. P. Příchovský is a group of sculpted figures by I. F. Platzer. The exquisite interior furnishings in late-Baroque style are also the work of Wirch. Note in particular the nine Gobelin tapestries, the wood carvings, the stucco decorations and the collections of porcelain and crystal. Ferdinand I bought the palace in 1562 for the Archbishop, recently returned to Prague at the end of the Hussite wars. It is still the Bishop's See today.

SCHWARZENBERG PALACE
Schwarzenberský palác

The building as it is today is in fine Renaissance style, clearly imitating northern Italian prototypes. Its designer, the Italian architect A. Galli, commissioned by the Lobkowicz family, carried out the work between 1545 and 1576. The external decoration, made with the *sgraffito* technique, looks exactly as if the masonry is clad in projecting pyramid shaped stones. The beautiful exterior decoration dates from the 16th century but was renovated between the 19th and 20th centuries. The Museum of Military History collections have been housed in the 16th century wing of the palace since 1945 and are exhibited in rooms of elaborate decoration. They include prehistoric weapons, arms supplied to the various European armies up until 1918, cannons, uniforms, medals, flags, military maps and plans of famous battles.

STERNBERG PALACE - NATIONAL GALLERY IN PRAGUE
Šternberský palác - Národní galerie v Praze

This Baroque palace is named for Franz Josef Sternberg who, in 1976, founded the 'Society of Patriotic Friends of the Arts', to which the members loaned their finest artworks. The collection grew over the years and was transferred to government ownership before World War II. The headquarters of the **National Gallery in Prague** since 1949, the palace has been the home of the **Collection of European Art from the Classical Era to the Baroque** since 2003. The first part of the exhibition is dedicated to Greek and Roman antiquities. The rooms on the first floor house works of art from the 14th-16th centuries from the collection of the Archduke Francesco Ferdinando d'Este, from Konopiště Castle, with paintings by Tuscan masters such as Bernardo Daddi and Lorenzo Monaco, works from the Venetian school (Vivarini's atelier) masterpieces and by the Florentine Mannerists, Bronzino and Alessandro Allori. On the same floor we can also admire the beautiful collection of Flemish paintings that include a triptych by Geertgen tot Sint Jans and a monumental altarpiece by. On the second floor are 16th-18th century masterpieces from the Italian, Spanish, French and Dutch schools by great artists such as Tintoretto, Ribera, Tiepolo, El Greco, Goya, Rubens and Van Dyck. The collection of Dutch and Flemish paintings is dominated by the works of Rembrandt, Hals, Terbirch, Ruydsale and Van Goyen. The ground floor features 16th-18th century German and Austrian paintings by artists such as Lucas Cranach and Hans Baldung, but the highlight is Albrecht Dürer's masterpiece, *The Feast of the Rose Garlands* (1506), that was brought to Prague by Rudolph II.

A collection of small sculptures, drawings and prints completes the exhibition.

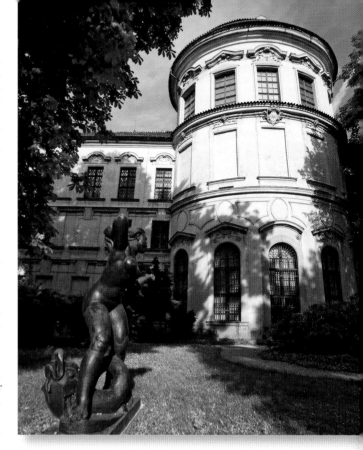

A corner of the Sternberg Palace and the gardens decorated with statuary.

A detail of the mighty colonnade on the Czernin Palace.

CZERNIN PALACE
Černínský palác

Now the seat of the Ministry of Foreign Affairs, the distinguishing marks of this majestic building are its imposing size and the massive colonnade which runs the length of the façade. The exterior of the ground floor is constructed with massive diamond-pointed rustication. Work was begun on the palace in the second half of the 17th century by order of the Ambassador to Venice, Count Czernin of Chudenice. It was completed towards the end of the century under the supervision of his son, Hermann Czernin. The many eminent Italian artists, including F. Caratti, who took part in the construction of the palace made some outstanding contributions. In the first half of the 18th century the adjoining **garden** was added, as was the magnificent stairway with its ceiling fresco by V. V. Reiner (*Fall of the Titans*). During the same period, F. M. Kaňka made some adjustments to the building. Towards the middle of the 18th century, following the French occupation, renovation work was required, and this was carried out by A. Lurago who added three doorways and rebuilt the garden *Orangery* in Rococo style. Around this time I. F. Platzer produced several sculptures which now decorate the palace halls. In 1948 Jan Masaryk, son of Tomáš Garrigue Masaryk the first Czech president, died here in obscure circumstances that remain a mystery.

THE LORETO
Loreta

The origins of this sanctuary, which ranks as one of the most visited religious destinations and places of pilgrimage in the whole of Bohemia, date back to the 18th century, although the legend which tells of the transportation of the Santa Casa from Nazareth to Loreto is much older (13th century). Following the Counter-Reformation, a great number of sanctuaries modelled on the one in Loreto were built in order to promote Catholicism in previously Protestant areas. The **façade** of the sanctuary was begun after 1721 by the Dientzenhofers, who had been commissioned by the Prince of Lobkowicz and his wife Eleanor Caroline. The main entrance is distinguished by the statues of *Saints* and the marble coats of arms which stand above it, all by F. Kohl. The Baroque bell tower houses a set of 27 bells (1694) which ring out in honour of the Virgin every hour.

A detail of the bell tower.

Santa Casa Chapel

This chapel was completed in the first half of the 17th century by G. B. Orsi from Como. It is located in the Cloisters, surrounded by porticoes and decorated with two fountains. The external decorations are either inspired by *Episodes from the Life of the Virgin Mary*, the *Legend of the Santa Casa*, while others represent *Prophets from the Old Testament* and *Pagan Sibyls*. The **interior** of the chapel, which was beautifully painted by the 17th century artist from Malá Strana, F. Kunz, contains an ornate silver altar, a wooden *Madonna*, and various silver decorations weighing a total of over 50 kg. The atmosphere inside is tranquil and enchanting; a splendid iconostasis stands before the image of the Virgin Mary. On either side of the Santa Casa are two 18th century *fountains* representing the *Assumption* and the *Resurrection*.

Left, the entrance to the Loreto Sanctuary on Loretánksé Square.

A detail of the cloister facing the Chapel of the Holy House – or Santa Casa - with the bell tower and the Fountain of the Assumption.

Cloister

The structure dates from the first half of the 17th century and is adorned with 18th century frescoes by F. A. Scheffler. The chapels surrounding the cloister are richly decorated with frescoes, paintings and sculptures, and contain wooden confessionals and altar frontals of excellent craftsmanship.

A view of the Chapel of Our Lady of Sorrows showing the frescoed dome and altar-frontal.

Below, the interior of the Chapel of the Santa Casa with the altar in the foreground.

Two images of the richly frescoed cloister.

Church of the Nativity

The construction of the Church of the Nativity, situated on the eastern side of the Loreto, halfway along the cloister, was begun by the Dientzenhofer father and son team in 1717, and completed by G. Aichbauer in 1735. The **interior** is a genuine triumph of Baroque, with its incredible wealth of decorations including sculptures, wooden inlay work, gold-leafed stuccowork, painted ceiling, angels and *putti*, and multi-coloured marble. The high altar is adorned with an altar-piece by J. G. Heintsch (*Nativity*), and the vaults are decorated with numerous frescoes including *Christ in the Temple* (V. V. Reiner, 18th century), and the *Adoration of the shepherds, Adoration of the Magi* (J. A. Schöpf, 18th century).

The lavishly decorated Baroque interior of the Church of the Nativity. Heintsch's painting of the Nativity above the altar is visible in the background.

Saint John of Nepomuk

Jan Nepomucký (ca. 1340-1393) was born in Bohemia; he was ordained as a priest and became the preacher to the court of King Wenceslas IV.

Recently historians have begun attributing his death to the fact that he opposed the royal appointment of an abbot, but tradition maintains that King Wenceslas wanted him to reveal what Queen Johanna of Bavaria had told to him in confession. Because he refused to violate the secrets of the confessional John was arrested, tortured to death and thrown into the river from the Charles Bridge (where there is a cross with five stars commemorating the crime). Still according to legend, five stars were seen shining above his lifeless body. Saint John of Nepomuk was canonized in 1729 and is venerated as a patron saint of Bohemia.

New World
Nový Svět

Not far from the Loreto complex is the 'New World', which is in fact a district within a district, and certainly one of the most fascinating areas of Hradčany. It is the students' and artists' quarter, a kind of 'Latin Quarter' on the banks of the Moldau, in keeping with the stereotype of the 'Paris of the East'. The former home of the astronomer Kepler ('The House at the Golden Griffin') can be seen here, as well as an attractive Baroque vinárna ('At the Golden Pear').

The hasty visitor can miss this narrow alley – a romantic and picturesque spot with Renaissance and Baroque buildings. An important element in many legends of old Prague, the New World is still a most fascinating place.

Strahov Monastery
Strahovský klášter

This building, founded by the Premonstratensians, dates from the 12th century when it was built under the patronage of Duke Vladislav II and the Bishop of Olomouc. In 1258 it was destroyed by fire and rebuilt in Gothic style. In the second half of the 14th century, Charles IV had the building included within the walls of Prague. It was considerably extended and embellished during the Renaissance, but destroyed by the Swedes at the end of the Thirty Years' War. The architect J. B. Mathey remodelled the monastery complex in Baroque style in the second half of the 17th century. Damaged once again by the events of war (1741), it returned to its former splendour in the neo-Classical period. In the early 1950s restoration brought to light the remains of the Romanesque foundations. In the courtyard there is a Baroque gateway, above which stands the *Statue of St Norbert,* the founder of the Premonstratensians. Rudolph II had the former Chapel of St Roch built in the first half of the 17th century; today it is used for exhibitions. Behind the 17th century *Column of St Norbert* lies the **Church of Our Lady**, also dating from the 17th century. Above the harmonious Baroque **façade** stands a *Lamb,* surrounded by the golden epigraph *Vidi supra Montem Sion Agnum.* The **interior** is divided into three naves and is richly decorated in Baroque style; it contains some fine furnishings (scrolls in stuccowork with images of the Virgin Mary). Next to the church is the part of the monastery which houses the **Museum of National Literature** (*Památník národního písemnictví*). The monastery's Historical Library, now once again in the possession of the monks (1992), contains 130,000 volumes, 5000 manuscripts, 2500 incunabula and a large quantity of antique maps. It also houses examples of Czech literature from the 9th to the 18th centuries.

The Library's **Theological Hall** is of particular interest for its fine stuccowork and its 18th century paintings. The barrel vaulting, clearly Baroque in style, is the work of G. D. Orsi of Orsini. The cycle of 25 frescoes by S. Nosecký, the Strahov monk, is a masterpiece in itself. The **Philosophical Hall** is of remarkable dimensions, corresponding to the size of the bookcases housed there. The large ceiling fresco was painted in the 18th century by F. A. Maulpertsch. Also on display in the hall is a *Bust of Francis I,* made in marble by F. X. Lederer in the 19th century. The most notable items in the library, those which constitute its wealth, are the valuable *Strahov Gospel Book* (9th-10th century), the *Historia Anglorum,* the *Schelmenberg Bible,* and the *Strahov Herbarium.*

The façade and the richly decorated Baroque interior of the Church of Our Lady.

Vyšehrad

"Vyšehrad" means a 'castle on the heights', and the hill where it is situated is said to have been the seat of the first Přemyslid princes.

It was almost certainly founded in the 10th century as a rival to Hradčany Castle. From the 11th century onwards it became more and more important as sovereigns established themselves here, and the building was expanded. It went into a period of decline around the mid-12th century, and was fortified two centuries later.

The settlement suffered greatly during The Hussite Wars (15th century). By the beginning of the 17th century the area had taken on the appearance of a Baroque fortress. After its destruction in 1911, Vyšehrad is today undergoing careful restoration work.

An interesting view of Vyšehrad from the Moldau.

CHURCH OF ST PETER AND ST PAUL
Kostel svatého Petra a Pavla

This church, situated on the heights of Vyšehrad, is a striking feature on Prague's skyline. Its twin spires dominate the houses which overlook the right bank of the Vltava, built by the Cubist architect, J. Chochol, making it one of the symbols of this quarter of the capital. The first place of worship on this site was built in the latter half of the 11th century. During the reign of Charles IV the church was rebuilt to become a three-nave basilica in distinctly Gothic style. It was subsequently remodelled in Renaissance style in the 16th century, and again in Baroque style in the 18th century. However, the church today offers the neo-Gothic appearance it assumed in the latter half of the 19th century. Further restoration work was carried out between 1981 and 1987, at the same time as some archaeological excavations. The **façade** of the church is wedged between two soaring spires, erected in the early 20th century and jointly designed by J. Mocker and F. Mikš. The neo-Gothic appearance of the façade is reinforced by its triangular tympanum decorated with sculptures. The lunettes of the magnificent, deeply splayed portals are decorated with mosaics (side portals), and with high relief sculpting (central portal). Note the doors themselves, enriched with coats of arms and precious gold-leaf work. The **interior** contains some notable frescoes with stylised motives, dating from the early 1900s. The church's charm is enhanced by the beauty of the decorations and paintings which completely cover the naves and the ceiling (which is formed of ribbed cross-vaulting). Pillars supporting ogival arches separate the three naves. Above the side altars, enriched with various works in wood (altar frontals, sculptures, triptychs), there are some finely illustrated windows. The high altar, by J. Mocker, is decorated with four statues by F. Hrubes (late 19th century); these represent *St Peter and St Paul, St Cyril and St Methodius.* Note also, in the first chapel on the right, the *Tomb of St Longinus,* an 11th century Romanesque stone sarcophagus, and in the third chapel on the right the 14th century panel painting of *Our Lady of the Rains.* Observe the fine wooden pulpit and the beautiful choir made of the same material.

CEMETERY
Vyšehradský hřbitov

Originally a medieval cemetery adjoining the **Church of St Peter and St Paul**, it was transformed into a **memorial** of Czech art and culture in the latter half of the 19th century. Famous figures buried here include the painter M. Aleš, the writers K. Čapek, B. Němcová and J. Neruda, and the composers A. Dvořák and B. Smetana. The sculptors B. Kafka, J. V. Myslbek and L. Šaloun are buried in the *Slavín Chapel.*

A view of the church interior with its abundance of decorations and paintings along the naves and on the ceilings.

Left, the beautiful façade of the Church of Saints Peter and Paul with its Neogothic spires dominates the silhouette of the Vyšehrad.

A view of the Monumental Cemetery, with the Pantheon (Slavin) in the background. The Pantheon was built in 1890 to celebrate the nation's glories and heroes.

Beef goulasch with dumplings.

Eating and drinking in Prague

*T*he cookery of the Czech Republic, and especially Prague, is rich and filling though in some of the most elegant restaurants it is quite sophisticated, and is derived from Austro-Hungarian traditions. As one would expect from a northern European country it is richly flavoured and high in calories. The most traditional dishes can be savoured in the characteristic small restaurants and in particular the popular beer cellars, much frequented by the residents of Prague, with their warm decoration and, especially their lower prices.

PRAGUE HAM
Usually served as an appetiser, this traditional cooked meat is renowned outside the Czech Republic too for its unusual smoked and spicy flavour. However, to savour this delicacy at its best you should ask for *uzené maso* – thick slices of ham cut by hand and served warm. Cooked and lightly smoked Prague ham originates from an old Austro-Hungarian tradition; it developed in Prague more than 150 years ago and then extended beyond the city. The ham is usually boned, left to salt for several hours in brine (water, salt, sugar and various spices) while the meat is massaged to absorb the flavour evenly, and is then pressed in a mould to eliminate the air, washed, dried, smoked and steam cooked. The meat is then left to season for 2-3 weeks.

POLÉVKA
The most frequent first course is soup – *polévka* – of lowly peasant origins, usually with a base of onions, cabbage and garlic to which an assortment of seasonal tasty and nutritious ingredients is added. These soups, served in steaming bowls, are naturally a winter dish and help to resist the rigours of the cold climate. There are many different recipes including potato soup (*bramboračka*),

Pork shin cooked in beer.

garlic soup (*česnečka*), sauerkraut soup (*zelňačka*), and the unusual dill soup made with buttermilk (*koprová polévka*); even more filling and tasty are the chicken soup (*kuřecí polévka s nudlemi*) or beef soup with liver dumplings (*hovězí polévka s játrovými knedlíčky*). Both bacon and pork rind are used as tasty dressings so it is no surprise that these soups – the only kind of first course in Czech cookery – are high in calories.

MEAT, FISH AND FRIED CHEESE
Meat is particularly popular and is eaten in abundance: pork (*vepřové*) is the favourite and is most frequently served roast with potato and sauerkraut dumplings. However, there are also many

Duck with apples.

Apfelstrudel.

recipes for the excellent local beef and veal (*hovězí*), usually roast or stewed and often served with a bowl of tartar sauce or other accompaniment (*omáčka*). A dish that really is worth trying is *svíčková* consisting of thin slices of veal served with Austrian noodles and a delicately flavoured cream sauce. Everyone who visits Prague must taste the spicy and delicious goulash which, although of Hungarian origin, is widely found throughout central Europe. This main course is made of beef cooked in lard with onions, peppers, tomatoes, potatoes and is well flavoured with paprika and cumin. There are also many tasty recipes in Czech cookery for game which is widely available (especially goose, duck and pheasant) and chicken (*kuře*). Fish is not as commonly found as meat, but many restaurants offer fine trout (*pstruh*), large carp (*kapr*, traditionally prepared for Christmas Eve, usually marinated) and salmon, as well as sea fish such as cod (*treska*) and mackerel (*makrela*). Lastly, another and rather original main course is fried cheese (*smažený sýr*), a savoury dish that is quite popular.

POTATOES AND DUMPLINGS
Although various vegetables are used in Czech cookery, cabbage and potatoes are standard fare and are most often served with an accompaniment of boiled rice or dumplings. Called *knedlíky*, dumplings come in all shapes and forms and are usually made of flour, potatoes or bread; delicate in flavour they are served in rich sauces and accompany meat or fish dishes. In general however, main courses are accompanied by sauerkraut (*zelí*) and potatoes (*brambory*) which are also cooked in various ways - boiled, roast, mashed, or fried - and may even appear in salads.

SWEETS AND DESSERTS
People adore sweets in Prague and especially around Christmas time cooks indulge their skills and fantasies traditionally creating dozens of different types of sweets and biscuits which tourists can buy from stalls in the streets. It is certainly worth tasting the nougat from Bohemia, small curiously shaped sweets which are decorated and covered with icing. Desserts of all kinds are enjoyed all year round. The pancakes (*palačinky*) are delicious, filled with jam, ice cream, chocolate, berries and whipped cream, as well as the pastry puffs filled with blueberries, plums or other fruits, and

Marinated beef tenderloin with dumplings.

the classic apple strudel for which there are various recipes using different kinds of spices. Lastly, other specialities are the walnut and rum biscuits, vanilla buns dusted with icing sugar and *vánočka* a layer cake with raisin filling.

THE HOME OF BEER
Historically this is the homeland of beer where, as the hop plant has always prospered in this area, it has been produced and consumed since the Middle Ages. There are many excellent varieties – also quite inexpensive – to be sampled in the characteristic beer cellars of Prague which one really should visit to understand the local character. Although all of excellent quality, the most famous beers are the traditional *Pilsner, Budvar and Staropramen*. In Prague friends meet to enjoy a glass of *piva* (beer) and to chat while sipping what is without any doubt the national drink. A visit to "U Pinkasů", near Wenceslas Square, is obligatory for the tourist; this little old beer cellar was founded by the famous sailor Pinkas who, as legend would have it, in 1843 tasted a delicious glass of Pilsner and decided to abandon his life on the seas to open a bar which is now so famous that it seems some 6000 hectolitres of *piva* are consumed there every year – magnificently flavoured and without gas as it is unpasteurized. Second to beer, the Czechs enjoy *slivovice* and then their traditional liqueurs. As for wine, excellent Tokai is generally available in Prague; although typically Hungarian, it is also produced in the Czech Republic in the area bordering Austria.

Plum puffs.

INDEX